A parent Alone
Antoinette Bosco

© 198_ Twenty-Third Publications. All rights reserved. No part of this book may be reproduced in any manner whatsoever, printed or electronic, without the written permission of the publisher. Write to Twenty-Third Publications, P.O. Box 180, West Mystic, Connecticut 06388.

Printed in the United States of America.

Library of Congress Catalog Card Number: 000-00000

Cover design by Bon Du Pre

Edited by Mary Carol Kendzia

ISBN 0-89622-062-1

Twenty-Third Publications
West Mystic, Connecticut

Printed in the United States of America.

Library of Congress Catalog Card Number 77-82903

Cover design by Ron Fendel

Interior design by Tom Kluepfel

ISBN 0-89622-062-1

Contents

Contents

Introduction

In 1971 I was asked by the planners of a local religious education congress to give a workshop on Catholic broken families. Since I was a divorced Catholic, raising six children, then from ages eight to 21, they thought I would be ideal as a leader for this topic.

My first reaction was surprise that religious education leaders had finally come around to recognize that Catholic broken families existed. But my second reaction was swifter and stronger. That was *my* family they were referring to. My family—a broken family?

I examined the premise. "Broken" means disrupted, no order or unity. It means to be cut up, displaced, not whole. I had known some broken families. Places where alcoholic fathers kept their children tortured in a prison of inconsistency, loving them one minute, beating them the next. Places where the livid anger of two parents was so deadly that children escaped from them via drugs. Places where a mother had so many lovers that her children had to be taken away and placed in foster homes.

On the other hand, what was a whole family? A place where there is a sense of unity and peace; where all the members of the family feel comfortable; where they care for each other, stick up for each other and would never deliberately hurt one another. That was the kind of home I had—not a broken family, but a whole family.

I responded to the invitation to participate in the congress by telling them, yes, I'd do the workshop, but only if the title were changed from "Broken Families" to "One-Parent Families," giving them my reasons for insisting on the change. They agreed, with apologies and enthusiasm.

Since then, I have worked seriously at attempting to change the broken-family image that plagues every family with a missing parent, and to help single parents *trust* that they can do a good and effective job of raising a fine family.

That's not to imply that the task of single parenting is easy. Not at all. Recently, the program director of a local Long Island television station asked me to put together what I consider some of the most important questions facing single parents. In doing this, I realized I was really listing some of the problems, as these questions show:

- What special authority and discipline problems develop in a single-parent family?
- Do the children suffer from the absence of a male or female parent as role model?
- Are there any advantages in this type of family?
- Are attitudes about single-parent families changing?
- How does growing up in a family with an absent father or mother affect the childrens' views on marriage?
- What essential strengths are needed by the single parent and where can these be found?
- What are the childrens' attitudes about the missing parent?
- Does moving into a single-parent setting create hostilities in the children, and if so, how can the custodial parent cope with these?
- Does the single parent tend to "overcompensate" for the missing parent, and if so, how and with what effect?
- Does the single parent feel guilt and a sense of failure?

What causes this and how can she/he get over it?
- Can single-parent family members have fun together?
- How does a single parent cope with loneliness?
- Is the single parent who has to be breadwinner, plus giver of all the other services needed by a family, in danger of succumbing to a personal energy crisis?
- In short, how can one person handle the burden of parenting alone?

When people ask me this last question, I pull out my sense of humor and answer, "With difficulty, great difficulty." Then I list some of the strengths a solitary parent must find—a confidence in self that admittedly gets shaky at times, but is strong enough to endure; good health; a high capacity for work so that you can handle many roles (breadwinner, chauffeur, cook, housekeeper, nurse, part-time plumber, etc., etc.) a strong will to keep you on course and prevent you from slipping into the deadly well of self-pity; and a strong sense of humor as a foundation for all the other strengths to remind you that you are only mortal after all, and were never meant to be a superperson.

In the past seven years, I have shared thoughts like these and much else of what I've learned about single parenting with many men and women in a similar position. More times that I can count, one of these parents has said to me in all seriousness, "You're a writer. You should write a book that would give us some help and the hope that we can make it as single parents."

Now I finally have responded positively to that request and have written this book which, I hope, speaks frankly and honestly about single parenting, dealing not only with the questions I've already raised but also pointing out that this can be a good life.

The subject of single parenting is escalating in importance due to the exploding numbers of such families and the changing social situation. Today's single-parent families are the first ones to exist in isolation from extended families. Moreover, they exist in an era of "liberated" womanhood and fractured authority patterns. The phenomenon of single parenting is not one of patched-up but rather, repatterned families which are developing a new structure of what family life can be, with no previously existing role models to follow.

When we get down to basics, however, all children need good parenting, and I am convinced from my experiences that good parenting is possible and is happening in many families with only one parent. I hope, after reading this book, that you, too, will share my conviction.

Antoinette Bosco

**Part 1
Accent on Family**

Tom Salver

Chapter 1
The Transition Trauma

Meet Evelyn. Her husband died after a two-year illness. The strain of those two years, added to the burdens of caring for their nine children, left her drained physically and emotionally. She is now trying to rebuild her strength and face life, but fatigue, fears and anxieties remain her enemies, giving her little peace.

Meet John. His wife decided that marriage and raising four children was not the way she wanted to live. She deserted them, seeking a different lifestyle, and left him with the children, ages five to 13. John, separated from his wife by her choice, not his, finds loneliness his biggest problem. "You come home from work, not to relax and talk to someone, but to start another full-time job," was the way he put it.

Meet Judy. She's 29 and has never been married. Two years ago she found herself pregnant after a brief affair with a married man. After a troubled period of examining her life, her values, her needs and goals, Judy chose to have and to keep her baby, a decision which radically changed her life. The focus of her time, her concerns, her money and her love is her young son. At times she panics at the enormity of the job she voluntarily chose. Most often she feels her new parenthood has helped her grow from a self-centered to a giving person.

Meet Rose. After two years of marriage, this lovely and lively 25-year-old wife became pregnant. Her elation at the thought of starting a family was crushed when her husband walked out on her in mid-pregnancy, saying he didn't love her any more. Counselling didn't help the situation. Rose is now legally separated, raising her 18-month-old daughter alone, living on $100 a month child support from her estranged husband, with $1300 a year from welfare to supplement this meager income. Her personality has changed drastically from the cheerful, outgoing young woman that she was. Now she is often depressed, untrusting of men, and mildly hostile to happily married couples. "Why me? What's wrong with *me*?" she still asks herself.

Meet Me. I was divorced after 19 years of marriage and have been raising my six children alone for the past 11 years. At the time of my marriage break-up, the children ranged in ages from three to 16. The responsibility of supporting the children as well as doing all the other tasks required to raise a large family became mine. After these 11 difficult years, I am finally beginning to relax emotionally as I see my children, now ages 14 to 27, happy, creatively productive and evidencing solid values. My life could be characterized as one of sheer pressure from the total responsibility of raising a large family alone, so much so that I haven't had time to be lonely—or at least I tell myself that. . . .

Evelyn, John, Judy, Rose and I are members of the fastest growing minority in the country today—the single-parent family. We are one of the 12.7 percent of the nation's families headed by a parent alone.

United States Census Bureau figures point out that 29 million families with children are nuclear, or intact, that is, headed by two parents; and 4.2 million are altered, headed by a single parent. The number of children under age 18 being raised in single-parent families total nearly 10 million. Of these, slightly more than 800,000 live with fathers, the rest with mothers. Some 90,000 children live with mothers who have never been married; more than six million live with mothers who are separated or divorced; and about two and three quarter million live with mothers who are widowed.

The surge in one-parent families is largely the result of a galloping divorce, separation and desertion rate. Widows, widowers, unmarried mothers who choose to keep their babies, and married people having spouses incapacitated by illness, physical or psychiatric disability, alcoholism or some similar serious disorder also account for a growing percentage of families headed by a single parent. Up until 1970, single-parent families having the largest percentage of children were headed by widows. By 1970 this had changed. Nearly 60 percent of children living in single-parent families had divorced or separated mothers, with 26 percent living with widowed mothers. The proportion of children living with mothers who have never been married increased in the last decade from five to nine percent.

What these statistics forcefully point out is that significant changes in child-rearing patterns are beginning to take place in 12.7 percent of the nation's families, having children who are minors. What's more, 4.2 million parents are facing the problems, crises, work and responsibilities of family life alone, without the support and nourishment of marriage; while some 3 million parents are part time visitors or missing persons in their childrens' lives.

Single parents have much in common. First is the obvious and basic similarity of being alone in the difficult job of raising children. Then, we are all trying to maintain the intactness and wholeness of the family. All of us have to contend with the image that we are less than what "normal people" should be. A diminished, negative image, though less severe than in the past, is still the heritage of the single parent. All of us have to develop new social lives, relying neither on couple-centered or "swinging singles" affairs. All of us have to rebuild our lives in this new situation, finding new self-direction, a task requiring a great deal of self-awareness, self-understanding and honesty.

Single-parent families come in so many different shapes, sizes and atmospheric conditions, however, that they are in no way carbon copies of each other. The major categories of differences are financial, the ability of the single parent to cope with the magnitude of the job, the ages of the family members, the size of the family, the education of the parent, and the cause of the single status. Even a cursory look at the different types of single-parent families points this out clearly.

Let's consider widowhood first. When marriage ends because of the death of one of the partners, the surviving spouse generally experiences a sense, not of failure, but of incredible loss, rupture and aloneness. The new single state is not one that is criticized. It is an act of God; everyone accepts the situation with empathy for the widow or widower. Thus, self-image damage is not severe.

However, everything else in the life of the newly single person is a shambles in varying degrees and for varying lengths of time. Widowed parents have suffered, unwillingly, severances from their partners, their roles, (often in the cases of women) their income-source, their lifestyles, their very identities. A study done at the University of Washington School of Medicine proved that the loss of a spouse registers a 100 percent stress impact on an individual, higher by far than the stress impact on people experiencing other very serious problems, such as divorce, retirement or pregnancy.

"The study confirmed what we have found here. The loss of a spouse is the most stressful experience an individual can have," stated a spokesperson for the Manhattan-based, Widows Consultation Center. The stress, of course, spills over to the family, affecting the children, who also are hurt, confused and made lonely by the death of a parent.

While widowed parents sometimes face financial disruption, legal tangles dealing with property settlements, insurance and such, their major problems are in other realms. They have to deal individually and as parents with loneliness, depression, the need to accept forced and major changes affecting their entire lives, and the need to deal with the pain which is their legacy when a loved one is suddenly taken away.

One widow said she was seriously depressed for months after her husband died suddenly. She believed she was experiencing only sadness until a friend helped her to see that the cause of her depression was anger—quiet and underground, but anger nonetheless that her beloved husband had been taken from her.

"Only after I faced the truth that it was anger, not sadness, that was keeping me from functioning, was I able to begin adjusting to the different life ahead of me," she said.

At the Widows' Consultation Center, professionals point out that one problem not well understood by friends and relatives is that there is no specific period of mourning for the widowed.

"Friends may say 'It's about time for you to snap out of this,' just as the widow is at the worst of her depression. This is her period of recoil and it is often very misunderstood. It may come a year or even several years after the death of her husband," said the spokesperson.

This is the time when the widow finally realizes that what has happened is an unchanging fact; she must face the finality of her husband's death, "and that is not easy." It is at this point that the widow is in the vulnerable and dangerous position of having her confused and sad state become a chronic one.

Widowed fathers also have to deal with mourning, depression, seemingly never-ending responsibility and both their loneliness and that of their children. One father said he realized the emptiness in his young daughter's life when she hugged him one night and said simply, "Mommy was so soft to hug."

Divorced parents have similar problems, but with enormous differences. For the divorced mother, the self-image damage is usually extensive. Initially, she wears "failure" as visibly as sack cloth and ashes, especially if she comes from a religious tradition holding to the absolute indissolubility of marriage. Everything converges to solidify this identification with failure, and in her vulnerable position, she can be disastrously shrunken into a diminished and weak person. She is no longer "at home" in the company of married couples; her church offers at best an anemic welcome; society shows its discrimination by refusing or making it difficult for her to get credit cards, car insurance, or a home mortgage. She is usually attempting to live on a low income, and in addition she often suffers the indignity of being considered sexually an "easy mark" by anxious men and suspicious women.

Her problems are compounded by the fact that as a divorced woman she must still deal with her one-time spouse, who perhaps is refusing to pay child support or is dropping in unexpectedly, disrupting the household. Moreover, the divorced parent-alone often has to cope with behavior problems in the children who have been damaged because of the parents' friction and separation.

These are the minuses, and the higher the minus score, the lower usually is the self image. Somehow, someway, the divorced mother has to find strength, renew confidence in herself, see herself not as a failure but as a person who has experienced a traumatic end to one way of life and now must pioneer—successfully—into a new life. This takes courage, determination, and sometimes "inspiration", which can come from faith, through another person who is kind and human and understanding, or even in accidental ways.

One woman said she was put back on a balanced course after listening to the words of the song, Desiderata.

"I kept hearing 'You are a child of the universe. . . . You have a right to be here' . . . It hit me that I had reached such a low point in my self-esteem that basically I didn't really believe I deserved to exist," she commented.

Divorced fathers usually have been thought of as the new Don Juans, living lives of bachelor freedom, fun and games, sought after by unattached women.

One divorced father said, however, "The truth is, I work and moonlight to help support myself and the kids. I go home to a two-room apartment that's stuffy and so quiet that I have to turn on the TV for company. I miss my kids. It's a sterile, lonely way to live."

He and many like him don't fit into the bachelor realm. "I was married for 15 years. I liked being married. I want a wife, a person who cares about *me*," he emphasized. "Imagine trying to build a new life with another person after putting 15 years into that other life. I'm too tired even to think about it," he said, and he looked it.

More and more divorced fathers are beginning to challenge what has been a standard practice in the courts—

awarding custody of the children almost automatically to the mother. Courts have always held tightly to the belief that children need consistent nurturing during their "tender years", under age 12. An important development among Family Court judges, however, is that this nurturing function, the "mothering", can be accomplished by father as well as a mother.

Not too long ago, a Manhattan Family Court judge awarded a father custody of his three children, ages eleven, nine and five, saying:

". . . Studies of maternal deprivation have shown that the essential experience for the children is that of 'mothering', the warmth, consistency, and continuity of the relationship, rather than the sex of the individual who is performing the mothering function." The decision in this case, interestingly, was made by a woman, Judge Sybil Kooper.

When you come to the bottom line, regardless of who wanted out of the marriage, who gets custody of the children, how well the adjustments are, and how positive the "new life" after divorce promises to be, the children are left disturbingly in the fragments of the old life. This statement can be challenged, argued, disputed, ignored—whatever. Nothing can change its truth.

The separated parent is in a uniquely upsetting situation, a neither-nor person living in a limbo of confusion. Is the marriage over? Is there hope for a reconciliation? The uncertainty of the present situation, the threatening future if divorce is inevitable, the change in the family finances, atmosphere, make-up—all lead to a serious state of dis-ease for the separated parent.

Separation is sometimes peculiarly looked upon by the courts. One mother of five had appealed for a separation from her psychologically disturbed husband who was keeping his children in a state of terror from periodic frightening outbursts of violence. After two months of deliberation, a judge ruled that she did indeed have cause for a separation. However, since the husband was making only $210 per week, it would be difficult for him to maintain two households. Therefore, the judge decided that a separation would be granted; however, the husband could remain living at home.

"What kind of a decision was that?" she asked. Ultimately she found the courage to borrow some money and move out of the house, the only way she could remove herself and the children from the damaging influence of an unstable father.

Sometimes couples who remain separated for a long period of time do reconcile. A young man, a close friend of one of my teenage sons, stopped by on a recent holiday to tell me that his parents, long separated, had reconciled. His father had walked out on the family eight years earlier, moving in with another woman. He had continued helping to support the family and saw the children occasionally. His wife, a lovely, attractive woman, got a job in a large department store. Her life became work, home and children; she never dated and rarely went out. Last year, the woman he lived with died. Out of loneliness, love, forgiveness, who knows, his wife took him back. The son said he was pleased about the reconciliation and having two parents together again.

Adjustment problems in families where parents are separated are usually complicated by the lack of finality in the situation. Psychologists say that positions of uncertainty, where decisions vacillate, are tremendously fatiguing situations for the persons involved. Children may find it much more difficult to cope with separation than with divorce or death which carry a finality. They accept the essential need to move forward, knowing for sure that the parents' union is permanently severed. When parents are only separated, children often speak in terms of "when" mommy or daddy "comes back." The separation situation is so fuzzy-edged that restructuring the family under such circumstances takes exceptional skills and emotional strength.

Single parents who never have been married are now coming out of hiding and growing in numbers, both due to and resulting paradoxically, in greater social acceptance of unmarried motherhood. Census Bureau figures show that illegitimate births set a record in 1975, adding up for the first time to 14.2 percent of all births in the country. Particularly large increases were recorded for women ages 20 through 29. The figures also indicate that the proportion of children living with never-married mothers increased during the 60's from five to nine percent. One follow-up study of over 200 unwed mothers, done six years after they had given birth and made the decision to keep their babies was conducted by the Community Council of Greater New York. Findings showed that single mothers are warm and demonstrative towards their children and follow society's childrearing norms.

"Six years after their first child was born, they have in most respects blended into the general population of mothers and children, and exhibit the wide range of lifestyles and life situations found among families in the population generally," said the authors of the study, adding that half the women in the survey were still single after these six years, and half had married, 50 percent of these to the father of their child. Of the non-married mothers, 31 percent had maintained contact with the father.

Never-married mothers still have their own tailor-made problems. "I often feel defensive, particularly when someone, unconsciously or deliberately (I'm never sure which it is) makes a remark like—'aren't you being selfish to deprive your child of a father? An adopted family would have given him two parents and so much love.'

"I tell them, sorry, no one would ever love my child as I do. If they can't understand the lifestyle I chose for myself and my child, that's their problem, not mine," said Sharon, who at age 26 owns her own house, has a professional job and is raising a son alone, with the help of babysitters.

Having a child without benefit of marriage affects dating relationships, said most of the single mothers I have interviewed.

One woman in her late 20's told me, "Some men are crude. Because you are, quote—an unwed mother—unquote, they assume that you're willing and anxious to jump into bed with them and actually seem insulted when you tell them to get lost. What's a little harder to take is that once I met a guy I really liked. I felt he'd make a super husband and father. But he said he couldn't bring himself to try to be a father to another man's kid."

Another trend in single parenting among never-marrieds is adoption. Single women and bachelors, too, have pioneered the path into becoming single parents—mainly of overseas children—through adoption. While these incidences still remain in the category of individual and unusual stories, adoptive single parenthood is now an available option and yet another indication that attitudes towards the structure of parenting have been decidedly altered.

The phenomenon of unwed mothers opting to keep their babies and raise them alone, sometimes with the help of relatives and friends, but rarely with the help of the father, is a new one which must be watched. The same applies to singles who adopt. If this becomes a trend, coupled with a societal acceptance of the capable woman or man who can manage to give a home to a child without the assistance or presence of a spouse, the impact of this development will be felt on the very institution of marriage and on the family-experience of ever growing numbers of children.

A final situation exists which is so ambiguous that often the parents and children involved would not describe their situation as a single-parent family. These are families fractured by the incapacity of one of the adults to function properly as a parent. A semblance of marriage exists, but without partnership. All the responsibility of keeping the family surviving rests in the hands of the non-incapacitated spouse.

These families are all around us, disrupted because one parent is alcoholic or has some other "sickness" such as gambling or a personality disorder; is in prison; is in a work position which keeps him away from the family for long periods of time; is physically disabled.

The functioning parent is in a hemmed-in situation which can trigger tremendous resentments. If this anger spills out, the children are doubly affected, first by the fractured family atmosphere, and also, by the sense of their powerlessness to help either parent. If the incapacitated parent is difficult, nasty or cruel, this usually has a devastating effect on all the family members.

Sometimes these situations improve; sometimes they deteriorate, but with the possibility of betterment still held on to; sometimes they're hopeless.

"My wife has been to an institution to be dried out three times. She comes back determined to stay off drink, but it doesn't last," said a father of three young girls. "My daughters need a mother. They're at that age. I keep going back and forth between being furious at her and feeling sorry for her. Whatever it is—this is no marriage, but I won't throw her out."

Sometimes you see tremendous courage in these married, but non-partner situations. Mary is one of the most remarkable women one could meet. Her husband has a physical illness which has shrunken a 210-pound man down to 80 pounds. He has been in a wheelchair for three years now. She dresses him, feeds him, cleans up after him, carries him from home to car to wheelchair so that he stays part of the family's activities. Last summer she drove from their home in St. Louis to New York City with her husband and seven children to visit her father and brother who is a priest in the diocese of Brooklyn. Few women would have had the guts to try such a venture. Mary has all the burdens of single parenthood, while facing certain widowhood, but because of her love is carrying these out with joy.

Parents trying to keep a family together in spite of a disrupted situation caused by an incapacitated spouse have to try to keep themselves and their children intact and growing while the walls around them are cracking. They need strong reasons and strong motivation for accepting the spouse and living with these conditions.

It is apparent that in virtually all cases, entry into single parenthood starts with trauma, a wounding reality that you are now saying yes to hard times. Where there was once a marriage, the wound comes from the surgery of being severed from what was or at least appeared to be a unity of man and wife. A once married person is less than whole until a healing process takes place. Raising a child or children with the total job on your shoulders is a frightening prospect, also part of the wounding. It's been said that a burden shared is half a burden; but a burden carried alone is the full weight, plus the half not being carried by a helper. Raising children alone does carry that added tax, most obvious when you look at the difficult and complicated job you're about to take on alone.

Children need to be nourished physically, emotionally and

spiritually. They need to be understood, to be treated with patience—love. In the case of divorced and separated parents, they need to be protected from the byproducts of their parent's one-time marriage so that they can be free enough to cope with their own burden of growing. They need to be young, to be disciplined, to be educated, to be given opportunities for creativity. The needs of children fill books, and meeting them is more than a job for two parents. Can one parent handle the burden alone? And if so, what kind of children will this parent produce? The answer is being shaped right now by over four million single parents.

Some sociologists are lumping all one-parent families under the new heading of "altered lifestyles" for modern families. That has the ring of lightness—in the category of the gay divorcee or merry widow. The day-to-day living in single parent families is far from light or gay or merry. It is emotionally burdensome, extremely lonely, and full of practical cares. It takes good health, a strong will, a ready sense of humor, and a high capacity for work to pull off being the solitary parent of a whole, not broken, family.

On the plus side, however, there are some gains. You have the joys that come from responsible parenthood; you have freedom and self-respect, knowing that in accepting your situation, you have chosen not to wallow in self-pity, but to trust in self and move forward, growing together with your children.

Chapter 2
The "Good News-Bad News" Scale

Every year when we hit a cold spell in January I remember, with a shudder, a January Saturday in 1968. It was one of the low points of my life. At that time, I was struggling to provide a wholesome home for my six children who then ranged in age from four to 17. My salary was $125 a week, which meant I did a lot of midnight moonlighting with my typewriter to support them. At the time I had bills, bills, bills and so I was depending on selling a number of magazine articles to keep financially afloat that winter.

Arriving in the January mail was an editorial response to one of my articles; it was both good and bad news. The editor liked my finely researched piece—about a program which was bringing black students from disadvantaged southern schools to spend their last two years of high school at Long Island institutions, living with volunteering families. The bad news was that he wanted at least 15 more photos and more quotes from the students themselves. He would pay $250 for the piece if I met his request satisfactorily.

In order to comply, this meant I had to reset interviews in four different villages and face another 150 miles of driving.

Still, the money would pay a month's rent, so I said yes.

The new interviews were set up for a Saturday which turned out to be the coldest day of the year. I had to leave my children alone at home, with the oldest ones in charge, hoping there would be no sibling altercations as they were all confined indoors on such a freezing day.

My work started with a complication. My camera attachment conked out and in the midst of getting people readied for picture taking, I had to run around trying to find a camera store to replace my defective equipment. I finally found a new flash attachment, shelled out $17 (the sum total of cash I had on me) and got back to work.

I finished by 4 p.m., hungry from skipping lunch, tired, penniless on the road, and concerned about my kids back home. As I started to drive, I found myself getting colder and colder before I realized that the heater on my old Ford Falcon had broken. Somehow, this was the final descent. My life started to hit me hard, and all of a sudden, for the first time in the two years I had been a parent alone, I was shaking with sobs, trying to keep the car on the road. Who needs this life anyway? What was it all about—never stopping for a minute to rest, working day and night for six kids who would never really know how much of my body and soul I had given to them? Life was just so much pain and discomfort and worry. At that moment, I truly wanted my frozen body to go numb and out—and never defrost again.

When I finally got home, I couldn't bend my fingers or feel my toes. I stumbled out of the car in the pitch dark, hoping my face didn't show the residue of tears. My daughter Mary, then age 13, greeted me with a hug. I could sense her relief that I was safely home. She had water near boiling to make me some hot tea, and a meatloaf in the oven. She had cleaned the house and kept the younger children peaceful. With these signs of love hugging me, my low point started to thaw and I was looking up again.

To me this has always been a good example of how the minuses and plusses in single-parent families can be balanced out. On the one hand, I was dealing with strong negatives that day—the need to be breadwinner, physical exhaustion, and conflict over leaving the children unsupervised on a Saturday. But on the other hand, I was experiencing the emergence of responsibility, consideration, love and achievement above expectation in a daughter who was yet only on the brink of adolescence.

From what I have seen in nearly a dozen years of contact with single-parent families, I have concluded that a characteristic peculiar to us is a pervading self-consciousness about our strengths and weaknesses, our advantages and disadvantages, our positives and negatives. We tend to weigh everything from the two perspectives of plus and minus; we feel enveloped by paradox; we battle a see-saw syndrome, pleased with our lives one day, displeased the next. Call this a supersensitive or up-tight condition, whatever. Labels don't matter. What does matter is equilibrium. The good-news-bad-news scale has to level off close to a balance, or the wholeness of the family is in trouble.

A few years ago, I asked my children to list what they saw as the advantages and disadvantages of being a single-parent family, both from their own experiences and from their observations of children from other such families. Their composite answers came out like this:

Advantages

1.   You don't have the business of playing one parent against the other.
2.   You don't have to watch one parent being dominated by the other.
3.   You don't have to watch your parents fight.
4.   It's easier to deal with one parental personality.
5.   You don't have to deal with the "difficult parent" on an everyday basis.
6.   It eliminates a lot of problems on decision making; one parent makes the decisions without being contradicted by the other.
7.   Growing with mother alone means being in an atmosphere with very little fear.
8.   There's more consistency with one parent.
9.   Children learn to become more self-reliant in single parent families.

10.   Children learn more consideration for parents problems.

Disadvantages

1.   You have a sense of "something missing"
2.   One parent is easier to manipulate ("If you're that kind of kid").
3.   A single parent has more work and burdens.
4.   There's not as much security.
5.   More boredom is felt in the family.
6.   There's not as much money.
7.   Kids feel "not quite normal" in single parent families.
8.   "Family fun" is a different thing from the kind of socializing you do when there are two parents; this is more important where there are younger children.
9.   The single parent feels kids should show more responsibility; the kids feel, "look, I want to be a regular kid."
10.   The single parent tends to be supersensitive about the fact that kids don't automatically show more responsibility.

Inadvertently, they had balanced the good and the bad and given me, and other single parents with whom I shared this, much to think about.

In the "disadvantages" corner, my children had placed a "sense of something missing" at the top of their list. Well, why shouldn't children "sense" this, considering that something very important—one parent—is missing from their daily lives? This absence manifests itself in many ways. One is boredom, also given a special mention in the minus column. In two-parent families, the added parent provides another source of energy, ideas and support for keeping a lively atmosphere in the family. A working, single parent has so much homework to do on weekends, it is extremely difficult to take the children on picnics or to ballgames or even shopping. The "monotony" of a parent constantly on the go to insure the family's survival is one of the burdens children, younger ones especially, have to learn to endure.

I remember a phone call I got at work from my son Frank a

few years ago and it spotlights the boredom problem. It was mid-February and the kids were off from school that week. A heavy snowstorm had come up suddenly, making the hills three miles away just perfect for sledding.

"Mom, could you possibly get off from work to take us sledding?" Frank asked.

I had to say no, sorrowing, particularly because it was the first time he had ever called me at work to ask a favor. He stayed home, shoveled the snow and built a snowman, and I loved him a bit more.

The "sense of something missing" is sometimes reinforced by prejudices our children meet. When Frank, my fifth child, was ready for Little League, I was then raising my children alone. In the town where we lived, Little League had one of those exclusionary rules that plague single parents. No boy would be accepted on the team unless his father participated as a volunteer. I protested the rule, arguing that it was unfair to boys without fathers. My two older sons offered their services as a surrogate father for Frank. Their request was denied. And so, Frank, who had no father to take him to ball games, picnics, fishing, swimming and so forth, was further ostracized by being refused admission to Little League. No wonder such children often become loners or losers, believing they are unworthy or abnormal. Fortunately, Frank was not so affected.

More and more research attention is being paid to fatherhood to determine how important a father is to children. Dr. Henry Biller, an associate professor of Psychology at the University of Rhode Island, and author of *Father, Child and Sex Role* did a study of third-grade boys, dividing them into four groups: early father absence before age five; late father absence beginning after age five; low father presence, less than six hours per week; and high father presence, more than two hours a day of father-child interaction.

Dr. Biller found that the high father-presence/interacting group achieved significantly better in academic performance and in their whole outlook on life than the others. The psychologist emphasized that an involved and interacting father is also important for daughters in developing a positive feminine self-concept. Clearly, he concludes, children are better off when they have loving, caring, interacting parents. When one parent is absent, no wonder children feel a "sense of something missing."

Another decided disadvantage in single-parent families is the enormity of the burden of parenting sitting solidly on one set of shoulders. The weight of the responsibilities are both in poundage and time. The work to be done is specific, sometimes unexpected, often tedious and conglomerately heavy. But worse, is the endlessness of it. You get no time off from parenting. No matter where you are or what you're doing, part of you belongs to the children, stays with them and keeps you unfree and preoccupied. The terrifying sense of "I'm all they have", and "If anything happens to me, what will happen to *them*?" is always a fear lurking somewhere inside you.

This trap can be defeating to both yourself and the family. Inadvertently, instead of leading your children to self-reliance, your immersion in parenting can delay your children's growth into independence. It can also subtly turn you into the classic s-mother-er.

When my oldest son, Paul, was a freshman commuter student at a nearby University, his transportation was a 1962 Rambler. One night I had just fallen asleep when the phone rang, about 11:30 p.m. It was Paul, just leaving for home from a late lecture.

"Mom, my car won't start."

My first reaction was anger that this had to be my problem when normally it would be in the box marked "father's job." But my second reaction was concern that my 18-year old son was unable to find his way home without the help of his mother. I got up, dressed, drove to the university and picked up my son. Just on a long shot, I said, "Let me have the keys a minute."

To Paul's embarrassment, the car started right up. He had apparently flooded the carburetor earlier, preventing the car from starting. Now I was angry again, feeling the absence of a father who would have given Paul a few lessons in car maintenance.

"You'll have to grow up, Paul. You can't depend on me to be your cab driver."

"I would have hitched, Mom, but you have a house rule forbidding this."

He was right, and I was solidly caught in the dilemma of my own making.

Overprotectiveness of this kind, plus a predisposition to worry and emotional stresses are easy visitors in the daily life of single parents, particularly mothers. This is a logical outgrowth of our own early maternal training. From the time our children are born, we watch over them, trying to protect them from all the things that could hurt them. We watch that they don't choke on their baby food, or crawl on dirty floors, or put saliva-soaked fingers into electrical outlets, or play with toys with sharp edges, or run into the street, or go into deep water until they can swim. I could fill a page with these "or's", and so could you, if you're a mother.

Most of the strain we feel, however, grows out of our situation. No one can be in two places at the same time. Who's watching the children when you're at work? No matter how adequate the day care or babysitting appear to be, your concern about the children is always decidedly frontal in your mind. When the occasional accident happens, your struggle to control guilt is almost as energy-soaking as your struggle for calmness.

When my youngest, Peter, was six years old, he fell out of a tree. I got the call at work from my daughter, Mary, Work, at that time, was 44 miles away from the house. She told me that a teenage neighbor had carried Peter home and the child was now lying quietly, moaning a bit, sleeping and apparently o.k. It took me an hour and 20 minutes to get home, dying all the way. Why hadn't I told her to call an ambulance? Why didn't I at least think to have her call on a neighbor for help? Did he have a concussion, a fracture, internal bleeding? Was I wrong to leave him with his 15-year old sister and not an adult babysitter?

As it turned out, Peter was shaken, but uninjured. My self-recrimination was that if Peter had fallen out of the tree when I was home, I could have provided him with immediate medical attention. Still, I reasoned, if I didn't work and had no income, Peter wouldn't have adequate food and shelter and then he would most certainly need medical attention.

I was playing the single-parent position of defensiveness in the vicious game of guilt, well known to most of us. We feel guilty because we have to be away from home to earn a living; because our children are deprived of one parent; because we have less of the material goods than we perhaps would like; because our houses are not spic and span clean.

Guilt and defensiveness are negatives and every single parent should recognize their unfairness and destructiveness. Instead of feeling guilt, we should be feeling *special* because we have found the courage, the guts, and the stamina to go out and earn a living in order to care materially for our children; because we are giving our children good parenting, even without the help of a partner; because we have understood that life and love are greater values than material goods; because our homes are comfortable, if not spotless. These are the good news nuggets which counteract the bad and go far in balancing the scale.

Two more of the items on my children's "disadvantages" list are interrelated—"not as much money", "not as much security." The security they referred to is non-material.

"There's something nice about having a male parent in the home. A father gives you a feeling of having something strong nearby. It makes you feel safer," said a 14-year old who lost her father six years earlier.

Mothers also were seen as security symbols by children being raised by fathers. They missed the special warmth and love associated with mother memories.

The security problem pops up often in the questions children ask, particularly young ones. Some of them worry and give voice to hidden fears by asking their custodial parent, "What would happen to me if you die?" or "If our house was on fire, would Daddy come and help us put it out?"

One woman, a widow, was having trouble with neighborhood children running through her yard and being somewhat destructive of her property. She heard her eight-year-old daughter holler at them one day, "If my Daddy were here, you wouldn't do that!"

"You know, she was right, and she was expressing something we all feel—a lack of security now that he's gone," she told me.

The lack of money is an even more serious problem. Most single parent families live on a severely decreased income after the change in the family, particularly if the split was caused by divorce or separation. The median income for families headed by a woman is $6400 compared with $13,800 for those headed by a man.

Today a notorious situation exists in our country where approximately one out of five non-custodial fathers simply refuse to make even partial child-support payments, in spite of support stipulations in divorce settlements. As a result, many families headed by a woman alone are forced to go on welfare. The Department of Health, Education and Welfare estimates that 1.3 million fathers are not making their child support payments, a defiance of responsibility costing society $1.5 billion a year in welfare payments. Most of these fathers skip out of the state where their families live, leaving no forwarding addresses. They literally disappear.

Two years ago, I was serving as a Human Rights Commissioner in my county. A group of women came to me asking for my assistance. They had formed a group called FOCUS, For Our Community And Us, whose goal was to move the courts and the legal system to do something about tracking down these errant husbands.

Their stories were sad, indeed. Most of them had dependent children needing supervision; had no skills, no training or education beyond high school; were unequipped to work except in a dead-end job at minimum wages.

"If I go to work, I bring home $80 a week. When I take out baby sitting costs, how can I live on that?" asked a proud woman in her 30's, detesting her welfare status and bitter against her deserting husband.

I went with this group's leaders to a meeting we arranged with the Administrative Judge of the Family Court. He was sympathetic, but said the problem wasn't his; it was in the sheriff's domain. We went to the sheriff and he said the problem belonged squarely with the county budget people. "Get me the staff and I'll try to help you find the bums," he said in his peculiar, colorful way.

In 1976 a federal law was passed to assist states in finding absent fathers and forcing the money out of them. This child-support enforcement law has to date established a nationwide locator service; permitted greater access to information contained in federal records, and stipulated that states without a parent-locator service must create one within two years. The FOCUS women tell me it all adds up so far to half a drop in the bucket.

"Women and children are much poorer in divorce than men," said one mother, in a letter to a daily newspaper in which she berated her county "where male justice prevails; where judges prefer to see mothers and children on welfare than fathers without enough to live on; where non-paying fathers are not subjected to judgments, sequestration, wage deduction or jail; where financial statements are never questioned or verified, and where more space is devoted to visitation rights than to support rights in the divorce decree." She adds, firmly, "Custody is not a prize to be won; it is a responsibility that is earned. Men who object to paying alimony and child support for children that are not living with them merely reinforce the argument that the mother is usually the better parent."

The money situation is a serious one, particularly because it generates bitterness, a negative, destructive force which can eat away at the responsible parent and spill over into the family, spreading its harm to the children.

If the discussion in this chapter has seemed to emphasize the negatives more than the positives, I plead guilty. The single-parent situation is so problem-laden that it is hard to lift oneself up and beyond them. I also know I've only scratched the surface of our problems, not having yet attempted to go into the effects resulting from the altered interrelationships between custodial parents, non-custodial parents and their children. That subject will come up in later chapters.

What I have tried to point out is the need to seek out the positives, in spite of the pervading problems. If a single parent has come to terms emotionally and financially with the new situation, then the way is clear for the positives to show through.

One of my biggest hangups was fatigue and a kind of suppressed, unexpressed anger that I had to work so hard. Often I would be no more than just inside the door when the barrage would start—"I need a ride to. . . .", "I need help with . . .", Margy's been a pain today . . ." I went through a brief period of listening, long-suffering, before I even got my coat off. Finally I realized I was being an idiotic martyr. I made two signs, one saying, "No requests for the next half hour," and the other, "Sorry, the deadline for all complaints was yesterday." When I entered the house, I walked in with my finger pointing to both signs. Without preaching or pleading, my message soon got across to them that I needed consideration after a hard day's work, and they learned to give this to me, appreciating my attempt at humor.

A decided advantage in single-parent families is the potential for peace. One parent is making the rules, the decisions; one parent is interacting with the children, eliminating discussion and conflict which often erupts between two disagreeing parents. About three years ago, syndicated columnist Ann Landers published a letter from a 12-year-old girl who said she was glad her parents had obtained a divorce. She wrote, "When dad was home, he and mom fought all the time and it made us very nervous. Mom had headaches and dad had stomach aches. Now they both feel fine and treat each other like friends instead of enemies. Us kids feel better too. My little brother has stopped stuttering and I don't shake like I used to when I was afraid my dad might lose his temper and slap my mother.

"So, kids, if your parents are separated or divorced, it probably means they had to do it for their health's sake and for yours, too. So cheer up and don't feel sad."

Most children will adjust to the new family style, even when the parental separation is due to death, if the atmosphere in the home is healthy, because as a tenet in the psychology books states: "There is an innate drive for normalcy in children." The healthy atmosphere, of course, must be created by the single parent, another topic to be discussed in a later chapter.

On another positive note, the old stereotype of the one-parent family being a "sick social unit" bound to produce damaged children, is fast being replaced with a new attitude viewing such families as "different", not "deviant." A physician, Dr. Saul Kapel, who also writes a syndicated column, (the *New York Daily News*) stated:

"Despite the problems and the personal tragedies of death, divorce, separation and desertion, most of the women of America who are 'mothers but not wives' appear to be doing an admirable job of raising healthy, mature youngsters, according to a recent report by the Office of Child Development of the U.S. Department of Health, Education and Welfare.

"The majority seem to be as capable of maintaining the virtues of home and family as anyone else, even though social disapproval, financial difficulties and the absence of a man in the house makes it more difficult for them.

"I am not suggesting that the loss of a father due to death or separation does not cause severe psychological and social stress for many children. It affects all of them to some degree. *But it is time to stop exaggerating these effects."*

It will be a while yet before single parents will be enough at ease with their situation to put down the magnifying glass. We will still continue to react in cinemascope proportions to all signs of weakness and problems, ascribing these to our single-parent status, even when the condition might simply be proper to any family. But if we work at trying to develop and recognize the bright sides, too, then the bad news can be well balanced off with the good.

Chapter 3
Authority-
The Bottom Line

The stories they tell . . . sometimes I think I've heard them all . . .

There's John, who has begun punching his little brother; Joan who's started wetting the bed; George, consistently a school truant; Henry, who has taken to night wandering; Peter, who's using four-letter words; Marcia, starting to dress like a tramp; June, loudly and rebelliously disobedient; little Jimmy, holding back on his bowel movements; Sandra, writing letters to her Daddy, promising to be good, if only he'll come back . . .

Meet with single parents, listen to our stories and soon enough you realize how the structures of our children's lives fall apart after the loss of a parent, for whatever reason. Most of us realize that we must build new emotional supports for our families, housing only one parent, but happy nevertheless. Most of us realize further that the new relationship we develop with our children is the crucial determinant in whether or not we're going to make it—sane, whole and happy—in our new roles as single parents. What many of us may not realize is the far-reaching effect of this relationship—how it heals and helps you grow when it is good; how it hurts and destroys you when it is bad. The happiest single parents I know are those building a solid, happy, positively interacting new life with their children. The miserable ones are those having problems with their children.

"I went to a psychiatrist and he told me I was tense and needed to learn how to assert myself more and let the tenseness hang out," said one mother, a nervous wreck over her inability to reach a misbehaving daughter. "I told him he was straight out of a textbook. My problems would disappear in a minute if my daughter straightened out."

I have no doubts at all that she was right.

I also have no doubts at all that single parents and their families are happy only when the new authority structure they develop is solid and working well. *For the authority relationship is what I see to be the major family function, since it determines both the direction of a child's growth and the values a child will absorb.*

Entry into single parenthood triggers a crisis, hopefully temporary, in the relationship between parents and children, brought on largely by the shift in authority patterns. Children, particularly young ones, are tremendously confused. Who guides them now, who do they obey, who do they listen to? It is as if they have a radio on with interference from two stations, and they can't untangle the mixed messages.

Think for a minute of what has taken place.

A child lived in a family where, on the surface at least, he had a nurturing mother and a supporting father—two loving parents, providing strength and security in his world. Now, one parent—in 90 percent of the cases, the father—is gone. The child feels the loss of security, which often brings on anxiety. He now has to deal in a different way with the remaining parent, who is usually undergoing severe personal strain. All of his in-house interaction is with this one parent, who now makes all the decisions, hands down all the rules, and has most or all of the responsibility for maintaining the family. The single parent, often immersed in emotional and financial problems, usually expects the child to be innately sensitive to her (or his) difficult situation. Very often the child reacts, not with sensitivity, but with anger, rebellion and disobedience.

As one mother said, after being called to school to discuss her son's terrible "acting out" with his teacher, "He's so angry—not at me, particularly, but angry *that* it happened—that his father and I couldn't make our marriage work."

This boy expressed his anger by refusing to conform to the wishes of his authority figures. Even very young children can express their anger when their family life is altered, aiming it usually at the remaining parent. One young woman who had to go back to work to support herself and her four-year-old daughter told me her child scowled at her every day when she picked her up at Nursery School. One day she refused to go with her. "You're not my mommy," she said. "You're just the lady who goes to work."

Instead of responding with guilt or defensiveness, the young mother answered, "No, I'm the mommy who *comes home* from work, because I love you." The child hugged her and the mother had made a giant step forward in preventing an authority conflict and increasing her child's loneliness and anger.

Setting new authority patterns is an immediate need in newly single-parent families, and, sadly, the need comes at a time when parents are often most unable to cope positively and strongly with their parental roles. A time of intermediate parenting occurs, lasting from a few months to about a year, and that time period can make or break the peace between the parents and children, according to a report in the *New York Times* (Dec. 31, 1976).

"Parenting practices are extremely poor in the year after a divorce," said Dr. Mavis Hetherington, a psychologist at the University of Virginia. "Mothers bark out orders like generals in the field but don't follow through on them. The fathers are going through the every-day-is-Christmas syndrome when they visit the children. And then they drop this indulged child off at the doorstep."

The fact that the father may be indulging a child is not necessarily positive. Dr. Mel Roma, a psychologist at the Albert Einstein Medical Center, finds that very often fathers who have infrequent visiting rights feel "devalued" and depressed. This is manifested by shortened and less frequent visits to the child, because it is painful for him to be with the child.

Children react differently to their new situations. Some appear to have no problems or difficulties; some don't agree that the divorce was for the best; some are angry that their mother got cancer and died; some are hurt, not able to understand why their father was killed in an auto accident; some, where separated parents still get together to fight, are exhausted from parental disputes that rob their energy; some are badly used as messengers between parents; some are afraid to express anger for fear of being abandoned by their remaining parent; some believe the break-up, and sometimes even the death, was their fault.

The negatives for a child losing a parent "far outweigh the positives", said Dr. A. Gardner, assistant clinical professor of child psychology at Columbia, and author of "The Boys and Girls' Book About Divorce." The applicable term, he said, is "sweet lemon—trying to make an asset out of a liability."*

Cruellest of all ploys used by conflicting parents who are each fighting for custody of the children is parental kidnapping. The scenario is bizarre and happening 20,000 times a year in our country. A parent, or a colleague, "snatches" a child or children, stealing them away from the parent who has custody. Unbelievably, the abducting parent gets away with the kidnapping scot-free. The law stays out of the situation, calling such abductions "family matters," not crimes. The Federal Kidnapping Statute, in its definition of a kidnapper makes an important exception. It excludes a parent who abducts a minor child. No legal machinery exists to enforce the rights of the parents left victimized, with no idea of where to find the child when such an abduction takes place.

In the past three years, some of the parents of the estimated 100,000 children kidnapped by a former spouse have begun to strike back. They have formed Children's Rights, Inc., a lobby group headquartered in Washington and organized to support legislation affecting the welfare of children. Meanwhile, what about the innocent victims of this drama—the children? What are they learning of life and values from their parents.

*(Report in *Newsday*, Dec. 7, 1973)

Special difficulties in adjusting to new interrelationships with children are felt by custodial fathers, who subconsciously or actually feel that taking over a role culturally prescribed for women is demeaning.

"When a male takes on the wife's duties, it has a negative dimension," said Emanual K. Schwartz, dean of the Post Graduate Center of Mental Health in Manhattan. "It is a comedown for a man to be a parent doing housework and child care. But it is not a comedown for a woman to go out and work."

How a father comes to terms with this role conflict is important in determining what his new relationship will be with his children and how effective his authority position will be.

In every situation where single parenting begins, serious readjustment is needed to counteract and heal the family disruption. Admittedly, the degree of adjustment varies, with some families finding parent-child relationships severely strained and others experiencing rather minor accommodations to the new shape of the family. But in every case, excepting, perhaps for never-married mothers, there is injury. No matter how positive the "new life" promises to be, the children first find themselves in disarrayed pieces of the old life. The place where this disruption is most evident is in the family's development of new interrelationships and new authority patterns.

The quality of the new authority in the family is absolutely crucial. For as I maintained earlier, I am convinced that authority is the major family function, the one determining the tone, direction and success or failure of our children's passage to maturity and wisdom.

Not too long ago I was giving a talk entitled "Is Survival Possible For The Parent Alone?". At the end of the question and answer session, an attractive, but troubled looking woman came to me privately and asked if I could help her. She was separated from her husband, raising three sons alone for the past year. In this time, her 16-year old son had become rebellious and disrespectful. He was leaving the house whenever he pleased, in defiance of his mother's orders. She had found marijuana in his room. She was desperate.

"I can't control him and I'm frightened. I know he's going to get into trouble. Whenever I try to talk to him, he tells me to get off his back and solve my own problems. What can I do to reach him?"

I suggested she try to find help through a counselling program. Obviously, the breakdown in roles and authority between herself and her son was beyond easy repair. The need for professional help was evident.

Authority-conflict can be the Waterloo for the parent alone, as it has been for this mother, or it can become a minor obstacle, positively overcome. From working with many single parents, I can say, with conviction, that most of the adjustment necessary in the altered family depends on how the custodial parent viewed authority in the two-parent situation, and how authority had been managed prior to the change to single parenting.

Usually I have found that authority problems with the children had a headstart in families where the marriage relationship was disruptive. A common trick used by children when parents are disunited is to pit one against the other. A young woman told me recently that she did anything she pleased before her parent's divorce because "whenever mom said no, I'd go to my father and tell him mom was being unfair to me. He'd then give me the permission I wanted. After the divorce, I never even bothered to ask. I just did what I pleased."

The girl was all of 14 at that time. Her mother excused the behavior by saying, "I couldn't control her. She was headstrong. I was just lucky she straightened out." She was, indeed.

Most parents couldn't live with such a laissez-faire attitude, and rightfully so, for the family will stay firm or crumble, depending on the authority structure. Authority is the crucial family function. It describes the interaction between parent and child which is concerned with the development of that child as an individual, teaching him or her to meet the demands of life with enthusiasm, leading the child to work on his or her own and eventually to act on his/her own as a fully formed human being.

Authority goes hand in hand with discipline, which should never be equated with rewards and punishments. Discipline means, really, to train the child so that the child develops his or her own built-in, self-regulating controls. Discipline has much to do with following a leader. The relationship between Jesus and his "disciples" expresses the idea perfectly.

Authority is often misunderstood and thought of as the right of the one in command to give orders to a subordinate. This attitude in parent-child relationships, especially in adolescence, can be fatal. The person exercising the authority is the crucial influence, determining how one will react to the "laws" and the "orders." The most important factor in authority is not the "what", but the "who."

This has scary implications for parents. It means we have to be aware that we are constantly projecting ourselves to our children. A saying warns, "What you are shouts so loud, I can't hear what you say." That's the real world for us, and as parents, we can only lead if we command the child's respect. With this respect, we can say "don't" comfortably confident that the child knows the "don't" is in his or her best interests.

Obviously, then, when the family structure is altered and parents find their lives disrupted, authority is in for a period of static, depending on how healthy and speedy is the readjustment made by the parent who gets custody of the children. The problems, as we have discussed previously, are multiple and severe.

The custodial parent has the extraordinarily difficult job of assuring that all the children also make a positive readjustment to the new family style, while carrying an unenviable legacy wrapped in questions: What was the relationship of each child to the now missing parent? to the still present one? How does each child view the break-up of the family, regardless of whether it has been caused by divorce, separation, death or fracture?

If the custodial parent is the mother, she often has brand new problems, some of which she is completely unprepared to face: Does she have to get a job to support the family? Is she physically healthy? Can she accept the shift in her role from nurturer to nurturer/breadwinner/custodial parent? Can she handle the full weight of responsibility in raising a family alone? Do her emotional needs, especially the need to be accepted and loved by her children, get in the way of her needed leadership in the family? Has her ego been crushed? Can she rally the constructive assertiveness she must have as a woman and a mother if she is to deal with her situation with strength?

Eleven years ago when my marriage ended and I was left alone to raise six children, then ages three to 16, I had to face these questions. I learned first that authority is threatened mainly by three problems which develop almost immediately in children shifted to a one-parent family status: anger at their parents; confusion usually stemming from their new insecurity; and independence, a belief that restrictions are now down and that having only one parent is synonymous with permissiveness.

How do you deal with these? In my case, I was determined that we would remain a solid, unified, whole Christian family. This could be done only if my children and I could maintain order, openness and trust in our relationships. We discussed and agreed on the following: that children need good, consistent parenting, whether it be given by two or only one parent; that the custodial parent must be recognized as being in charge, with the responsibility of setting limits for behavior; and that responsibility is mutual in any family.

I further felt that the wholeness of our family could be achieved only if the authority relationship I had already set up with the children was good—and this would now be tested; and only if I remained strong enough to handle the multiple demands of my new role. One plus that I—and any single parent—could capitalize on was the knowledge that my word was *it*. Without another parent in the house, no vehicle existed for the children to attempt to "divide and conquer."

I learned soon that the saying "different strokes for different folks" applies very strongly to children. Where one daughter (13) expressed a sense of "relief and peace" after the divorce, one son (15) saw "failure." He read the breaking up as an inability of his parents to solve their problems and consequently claimed independence from them and their authority, manifested by school truancy. A school counsellor worked with me to help my son understand that divorce is sometimes the only way—and thus, the successful way—for people to solve their problems. Another daughter (11) reacted by expecting that she would have unlimited freedom to do whatever she wanted. She informed me she was sleeping at a girlfriend's house one night, babysitting another, and going to a carnival on a third. I said "no way." She pouted, but over a chocolate sundae—just the two of us—we became friends again as she heard me spell out *my* limitations, the things I could take from the children and the things I would not tolerate.

Positive steps were also important in trying to permeate the environment of the home with order and love. At times I found help in unexpected places. One of these was a chance reading of a novel called "Franny and Zooey" by J. D. Salinger. The section that struck me was where the mother, concerned about her daughter's health and anxious to reach out with her love to heal, offers her daughter chicken soup. The narrator sees the act as an offer of *consecrated* chicken soup, an act made holy by the mother's love. Beginning then and for years after, our grace at meals was punctuated by "And tonight we're having consecrated stew (hamburger, fish . . .)" My children and I never ate a meal together without being conscious of our love. Corny? Maybe, but effective.

My experience has been that when your love comes through, even in spite of other discontentments, the authority relationship works out positively. I can say this since all but one of my children are now adults, good people, very creatively engaged in their chosen work. But let me underscore that good results come only from consistent hard work, the willingness to pick up and go on after failures, strong faith and some good luck thrown in.

If I were to give "guidelines" to a single parent, these are the important tenets I would include:

Make very few rules. As a parent alone, you don't have the luxury of time, and it takes time to keep check on whether rules are being followed. The more rules, the more time required, and the more rules to be broken. I have always had just one basic rule in the family: No one was allowed ever to be deliberately cruel or unkind to any person within or outside the family. This meant that certain restrictions were implicit.

For example, my daugher Margaret hitchhiked to the beach one summer when she was 15. When she got home, she was made to understand how she had caused all of us to suffer from worry. She had broken the basic rule and she accepted her punishment of being "grounded" for a month.

I never made rules about curfews, homework, bedtime hours, use of my car or telephone, dating, etc. Each occasion was negotiated with the child, depending on the circumstances. This developed a mutual respect, and only rarely did one forget to call me if he or she would be coming home later than our agreement.

Never give an order unless you intend to follow through. One single mother told me that she's constantly "barking" orders to her children and they go right on doing as they please. Her excuse for not following through was that she's "too tired." Single parents have to avoid the trap of feeling beaten down, because in that position, the children, literally, walk all over you.

Make sure your children are properly supervised. Two single mothers I work with have 10-year-old daughters at home, alone for five or six hours a day. Both have started rebellious behavior. A few years ago I was interviewing a Family Court judge who said she was seeing more and more children under age 13. "The problem is not broken homes," stated Judge Maria Santagata, "it's lack of supervision." From my observations, I have concluded that a major cause of authority conflict in one-parent families is the result of a child having been left unsupervised too often at an early age. Subsequently, the child develops a premature independence and unwillingness to be "told" virtually anything.

Along with these basic controls, there are other truths to be aware of, like, don't kid yourself, there will be stress times; be consistent, fair, honest; stay in good health; and keep a sense of humor.

Above all, never forget that a single parent doing a good job is always undisputedly better than two parents doing a poor one.

Chapter 4
Overcoming Powerlessness

- Marie couldn't believe it when her husband told her after 11 years of marriage that he was bored with her, had met another woman who had given him a new interest in life, and that he was leaving her. She cried, she begged, she pleaded with him to reconsider what he was doing to her and the three children. She warned him that she wouldn't be able to cope, that the kids would be damaged, that he was throwing away the lives of four people. He left, anyway, agreeing to support the family. Within a year, Marie had to sell the house, because she couldn't handle the upkeep on it and it was getting shabby and in need of repair. She and the children moved to a two-bedroom apartment and live somewhat withdrawn from neighbors. She thinks her problems will only go away if she marries again.

- A woman attending a meeting of Divorced and Separated Catholics started to cry as she told of her predicament. Her neighbors were forbidding their children to come near her house or family because they said her ex-husband was "crazy." They didn't want to take a chance on having their children bump into this man they considered weird.

• One widowed mother of four young children stays on the phone all day long calling her relatives with the same constant complaint. She didn't bargain for this kind of life. She was supposed to have a husband and a father for her children. God wasn't being fair with her.

• The young woman is in her 20's, raising a two-year-old child with her mother's help. Her husband left her suddenly, without explanation. She feels she should get some education and training and get a job, and to date, she has paid for and started four different courses and programs. She has dropped out of every one, long before completion.

• This man has been deserted by his wife who took off with their two young daughters. She left him to raise two young teenage sons. He feels the 13-year-old is constantly being disobedient. To punish him, he called a local Family Court judge to complain about his son, forcing his terrified son to sit and listen to him while he talked to the Judge.

• A school psychologist called a widowed father caring for seven children, suggesting that since his income was low and he left the children to be cared for by his 12-year-old daughter, the children would probably be better off in foster care. The father is now a nervous wreck, worried that "they'll" take the children away from him.

• In another family, a mother, separated from her husband, has three elementary-school-age children who are constantly ill or injured and frequent visitors to doctors and emergency rooms. She constantly vocalizes that their illnesses are all due to the fact that her husband left her to do a job she can't handle alone.

• A 16-year-old girl keeps calling her policeman father who has been separated from her mother for the past six months, at work, pouring out her problems to him. She's gotten to the point where she's virtually afraid to act, without being able to say, my father, the policeman, said it's o.k.

All of these are true situations I have encountered over the past few years. All of them point out one of the most serious negatives overtaking families when they are altered to a single-parent status. The condition occuring is a cessation of normal growth, an inability to move out of a fixed position which in some way is a scream of anger and hopelessness.

The best way to describe this condition is to call it exactly what it is—a family suffering the loss of *power.*

The power I'm referring to is not force, or might or clout. It is power in the sense of its root meaning—*to be able;* the potential to cause change when this change is needed and constructive; to prevent change when this change is negative or destructive.

I'm referring to power as the potentials given to every one at birth, which become a collective, stronger force when combined in the community called family.

Psychologist Rollo May* said, "Power (is) the birthright of every human being. It is the source of his self-esteem and the root of his conviction that he is interpersonally significant. Whether a person is black or a woman or a convict or a patient in a mental hospital . . . the problem is roughly the same—to enable the individual to feel that he will be counted, that he has a valuable function, that ;'attention will be paid.' "

Dr. May called power "a fundamental aspect of the life process" while admitting it is a misunderstood term.

"As soon as powerlessness is referred to by its more personal name—helplessness or weakness—many people will sense that they are heavily burdened by it," he says.

My observation has been that all too many single-parent families fall, sometimes briefly, sometimes for too long a time, into a condition of weakness, brought on by their own or society's attitudes towards such families. The aura in the family is one of loss—loss of a parent, status, comfort, money, friends, social life, security. The result is a sense of less—less important, worthy, dignified, productive, upwardly mobile. The combination of loss and less adds to a sense of powerlessness that must be overcome if the family is to grow in health and wholeness. The single parent goal must be to begin a new process where this family is seen as a healthy, stabilized unit, not defective or deficient. To achieve this goal, the family must restore its power, firmly and clearly expressed as *must do, can do, will do.*

The loss of power in the altered family is manifested in many ways, particularly in questions: What is happening and why is it happening to us? What's wrong with us? Who can we influence now? What do we count for? Who cares about us?

*Rollo May, *Power And Innocense,* W. W. Norton & Co., Inc., New York, 1972

Who's noticing us? Can we survive alone?

The single status itself is most often caused by a traumatic happening—the death of a spouse or the death of a relationship—which requires survival on the part of the afflicted spouses. After a reasonable mourning period, if a person doesn't emerge from this dreary, but necessary, state, the mourning usually makes the transition to depression. An individual, or a family, undergoing any degree of depression is immobilized and thereby powerless to embark on constructive growth.

A major change in new single-parent families shows up in the family's attempts at socializing. I and every single parent I have ever talked to have experienced to some degree the actuality of being shut out of parties, get-togethers, socials, dinners, and so forth, which were once very much open to us. Often the excuse is made, without apology, that "We didn't think you'd be comfortable with everybody else being a couple." Mainly, that translates into, "We don't want an unattached woman around—or her kids, either, for that matter. Our husbands attention should be on us and *our* children."

This ostracism can erode a family's sense of power because it defines the single-parent family not as a positive functioning unit in itself but as an entity having an existence only as it relates to the other families—a definition which comes out negatively threatening. This social ostracism can puzzle, hurt and cause a single-parent family to isolate itself from neighbors and former friends.

In his book "Creative Divorce", Mel Krantzler* quotes a woman named Helen. "I get the strong impression," she says, "I'm some kind of pariah. The other day I was at the store and spotted the mother of one of Jimmy's classmates, whom I had gotten to know through the PTA. She actually ducked behind a display of gardening equipment to avoid having to talk to me. It's getting to be a pattern. This town is like Noah's Ark: If you aren't part of a pair, they shut you out."

The author adds, "Helen feels that because of these experiences, she is spending more and more time by herself. 'It's getting so I prefer my solitude, lonely as it is. Last night I

*Mel Krantzle, *Creative Divorce,* M. Evans & Co., 1973.

stayed up until three o'clock trying to sort out in my mind just where things went wrong. I even tried writing down a list of the main points, but I haven't got it straight yet'."

Choosing solitude, as Helen is doing, can be constructive if it is temporary and leads to a sorting out of goals and values in embarking upon a new single life. But if solitude is used as an escape from action and pain, as a quest for protection from the world and its hurts, then this is only another method of descent into powerlessness.

Children feel a sense of abandonment keenly after the loss of a parent, with their sense of powerlessness proportionate to their degree of dependence on the now-gone parent. The family upheaval is terrifying because the child senses that his at-home parent is feeling vulnerable, inadequate and threatened, and worries that this parent, too, might abandon him. Children are unequipped to handle significant estrangement. The death and divorce "demons" plaguing children need to be exorcized, say the psychology experts, but is the single parent actually capable of doing this and laying the groundwork for future family stability and family health?

If the parent is in an immobilized, powerless state, the harm soon shows up in the children. If the parent has been unable to communicate to the child that he or she has worth, the danger exists that the child will bypass a crucial stage of growth—self-affirmation—which Rollo May calls the "constructive assertion of the power to be." He or she will jump from his powerlessness straight into aggression, possibly hostility and maybe even violence.

A prison chaplain told me that most of the juvenile delinquents he deals with in the Children's Shelter, who have a record for violent behavior, usually say that they got into trouble because they were "hanging around", "had nothing to do", "were bored." All those expressions indicate undeveloped power—potential left dormant. When constructive assertion of one's powers remain frozen, you can be sure an unconstructive reaction will fill the void.

The harm caused by the loss of power in altered families is manifested both in ways common to many of the families, and in results shaped by the individual situation of the particular family, as the true stories at the beginning of this chapter pointed out.

Most common damage is seen in families characterized by dissatisfaction, tension, depression, anxiety, panic and jealousy. The family environment created by this mixed bag is absolutely poisonous. No way can a family find its new potential for growth and health while encapsulated in these traps.

The key question then becomes, how do you get out of these traps? How do you overcome this sense of powerlessness in yourself and family?

In the 60's, we saw the emergence of two movements, Black Power and Woman Power. In the 70's, we're hearing of Senior Power. These rallying cries came from dispossessed groups who believe that if power is to be theirs, if they can effect any change in their positions, it will have to come because they demand it, assume it, take it.

The single parent family also goes through an initiation period of being disposed—feeling itself to be an ill-fitting entity, no longer a member of the former two-parent family society, and not yet an independent, functioning organism generating its own power to grow. But power it must have. It need not, in fact should not, be militant; but it must be recognized, sought after and assumed.

The responsibility for this belongs mainly to the single parent and the place to begin is with his or her own life, outlook and goals. Contrary to popular negative beliefs about working mothers, the mother who sparks up her education and gets a job stands a far greater chance of getting her family's power restored than does the mother who resists this change in her life. I can give endless numbers of stories about families being rapidly energized because the single parent refused to drop out of the flow of life, came out from behind the four walls and got interested in something other than self.

My friend Mary is a common denominator example. An R.N., deserted by her husband and left to raise three children and an infant by herself, Mary got a job as a Public Health nurse in her county and later signed up at a local university nursing college to earn her baccalaureate degree in nursing, part-time.

Working, going to school and taking care of a family is difficult, but it's being done all the time. I did it myself while getting a Masters Degree and no way would I underestimate the amount of effort and energy it takes. But it has rewards in the sense of accomplishment you feel, in the pride in you expressed by the children, in the knowledge that you used your potential to move yourself and your family forward. I work in a university and constantly meet working single-mother-students from their early 20's to mid-50's. They've restored power in their lives and in their families.

One of the most effective ways for single parents to overcome the sense of powerlessness in their families is to get assistance from agencies and groups of both varieties—outside help and self-help.

Outside help is available through agencies like Catholic Charities, Family Service Leagues and Mental Health Clinics. Families experiencing problems which have pathological overtones should certainly seek this kind of outside professional help. Examples of situations indicating the need for such counselling or therapy would be:

• severe depression, where the parent, or a child, is tired, unable to find interest in anything, unable to function and carry out ordinary, required duties; is prone to crying easily and listlessly asking, who wants to live, anyway?

• overt and deviant misbehavior in one or more of the children, leading to delinquent or criminal acts, such as repeated truancy or stealing cars;

• escape from reality by a family member who has resorted to a dependence on drugs, from valium to barbituates, to alcohol;

• excessive nervousness or confusion of a family member, affecting the ability to make decisions, relate well with others, to sleep or eat properly, negatively affecting normal productivity;

• severe anxiety, causing unreasonable fears and blocking normal functioning.

The majority of single-parent families have manageable crises and need only the strength of camaradie to help them overcome their initial sense of powerlessness. I have worked for several years **with groups of** divorced and separated

Catholics and the repeated testimony of those who come seeking self-help is massive relief at finding they aren't "freaks" or "hopeless cases" or "unique" or "worthless." The knowledge that a lot of us are pioneering this new family lifestyle together gives encouragement and stimulates courage. Time and again, I have marvelled at the change in just a very short time which I've seen in men and women coming to these groups. They qualify for "before" and "after" stories, having moved from weakness—powerlessness—to strength—power.

Two of the most popular self-help groups are Parents Without Partners and MOMMA. PWP was the original national group for single parents, offering psychological help and a social corner for them to call their own. It has some 500 chapters and 100,000 members. It also has an offshoot now called Young Single Parents.

MOMMA came into being in 1972, started by some single mothers in Los Angeles who felt that the mere act of organizing themselves would help reduce the isolation and frustration they felt at trying to raise their children without the help and companionship of mates.

"Our idea is to build a community of women who can talk with each other without having to explain themselves," said a divorced mother of three, quoted in a 1974 *Parade* interview.

MOMMA has become an action group, getting involved in projects geared for parent re-education, parent effectiveness and co-parenting, in which divorced or never married couples are helped to work out joint custody or mutual parenting of their children.

In Manhattan, a private club for single, widowed and divorced men, called the Sword Foundation, was established in 1963 and has over 100 members at any one time.

"We are not here to commiserate with each other. We are here to have a good time. We get healthy by doing, not by crying," stated Dr. Irving Miller, the only original founding member still single.

Dr. Miller well expressed why self-help groups are effective. By rejecting tears, self-pity, commiserating—all dead ends—and stimulating *doing*—movement, growth—they motivate and propel single parents out of powerlessness into power.

In my own family, I was determined from the beginning of my single parenting that we would not be stigmatized, immobilized or in any way negatively affected by the change. I recognized that the descent into powerlessness was subtle and swift, called this the enemy and said *no*.

The first and immediate step I took was deliberate and symbolic of my conviction that we could create our new family if we were willing to run some risks. I moved out of the house and suburban community where we had lived for 11 years and into a new village, where we could have a fresh start away from all references to the past. This was difficult at first for the children, because it meant leaving their known schools, their from-babyhood friends. It meant financial jeopardy for me and the need to increase my income substantially at a time when much of my energies would have to be spent on parenting itself and assisting my children to adjust to a new environment. But we did it, and it was right. It was an overt rejection of powerlessness.

The societal factor which turned out to be the most devastating to me as a single parent was the school. Guidance counsellors, principals and teachers were overly conscious of the "home situation", and I found a tendency to read every aspect of my children's behavior as due to the lack of a father in the house. If they misbehaved, it was for lack of a father's discipline; if they did well, it was their reward for overcompensating their lack of a father in the house.

I challenged and fought that prejudice. One incident involved a call from a guidance counsellor when my daughter Margaret was in ninth grade. She said Margaret was very nervous and uptight and maybe I was "over pressuring" her because I was trying too hard to be father and mother, too.

"No," I told her. "I have observed the same thing in Margaret, but the pressure is coming from school, not home."

We looked into the situation immediately and discovered that Margaret, beautiful and bright, was being harassed by a gang of five not so beautiful and bright 10th-grade girls, who did nice things like spill their lunches all over her, and threaten her with beatings. Margaret hadn't told me because she didn't want to give me added burdens.

I took Margaret out of that school, got her enrolled in a Catholic high school, accepting the inconvenience of tuition and travel (the school was 25 miles away from our home). She had a beautiful two years in that school, graduating with honors after only three years of high school.

With this move, my children and I reinforced our power by asserting our ability to call our own shots.

Another incident involved my son Peter when he was in fifth grade. His male teacher was "old school", using text books so outdated that they had to be scotch-taped together. He believed in homework, too, the boring, non-creative time-wasting nonsense of writing each word 100 times, etc. I felt Peter had more valuable things to do with his time away from school, the only hours of the day he could devote to any creativity or mental stimulation. Still, I tried to get him to conform, hardly getting excited when he turned in incomplete homework assignments. Finally, the teacher called me at work one morning to complain that Peter was failing homework. I argued that writing the word "fish" 100 times, his previous assignment, seemed to have very little to do with learning. His response was—

"What Peter needs is a father who will give him a good beating. Then he'd get his homework done."

"Mr. T.," I said. "I have raised six children and have never laid a hand on one of them. I'm not about to change my style or my values now."

I also told him that I believed an educator is one who excites a child with the joy of learning, and in no way could I ever equate beatings and force with constructive education.

What the man had tried to do was intimidate me, put me on the defensive and propel me to accept *his judgment* that Peter was somewhat handicapped, coming from a deficient family lacking a father and being led by a permissive mother. I wouldn't buy. We were a family asserting our potentials. He must have gotten the message. Peter passed.

How do you know when you have emerged as a family out

of powerlessness and into power? The signs are all around you. You have stopped concentrating on your deprivations and are conscious now of all you have; you have stopped making excuses for yourself and your family; you stride in confidence, giving up defensiveness; you communicate well with others; you are productive; you begin to check off successes.

The high point for me came in 1973 when I was asked by the Christian Family Movement to lead two workshops on Single Parent Families at their annual convention to be held that year at Notre Dame. I thought about the offer, asking why would anyone want to hear what I have to say? I could tell them anything and how could they disprove it? What would make the workshops real would be to have the people attending talk with and listen to me and my children together as a family. I contacted the leaders and told them yes, on one condition, that we do the workshops as a family. They were delighted with the change. My four youngest, then ages 19, 17, 15 and 10, were on the program with me (my two older boys had summer jobs and couldn't leave). Naturally, they got all the attention. I was right. The parents attending wanted to hear their testimony, not mine, that single-parent families could be intact, solid and loving. That week I knew with certainty that we had not capitulated into powerlessness. We had our house in order, with the power *on*.

Evidence is growing that most crisis situations are overcome not instantaneously, but in stages. Certainly, this holds true for newly altered families. Stage 1 is the *mourning* period, rising after the death of a person or a relationship; stage two is *guilt,* blame turned inward; then follows *anger,* an outwardly-focused resentment or fury that this unwanted and undesirable thing has happened to you; a period of *realistic sadness* overtakes you as anger subsides. If this does not degenerate into self-pity, then you are ready for the next stage, *re-equilibrium,* which puts you in the position where you can now begin new growth. The final stage is the *renewed sense of power* which comes after new growth begins.

This is the possibility. It is up to the single-parent family to actuate this possibility. Interestingly enough, another definition of power is exactly that—moving from possibility to actuality.

Chapter 5
Creating Trust Between Parent and Child

Shortly before Christmas I was visiting my friend Pat, who like myself is a mother alone. She has only one child, Bobby, a sweet kid, 11-years-old, creative and bright in school. Bobby is very interested in science and was hoping to get some scientific equipment for Christmas. When his father suggested a microscope, the sixth grader said "wow" and began to hope.

The day I was visiting Pat, a week or so before Christmas, Bobby's father had called to say he purchased the microscope but had changed his mind about giving it to his son.

"I've been trying it out and I'm having so much fun with it, I decided to keep it for myself. He's probably too young to take care of it anyway," he said, without apology.

On Christmas afternoon, he visited Bobby and handed him an envelope with ten single dollar bills in it. Bobby hid his disappointment by thanking his father for the money, handing it to his mother and then excusing himself to go to his room until his father left the house.

He would "forget" this in the same way he has forgotten the time his father took him out to go bowling, but detoured to visit a lady friend, leaving Bobby alone to sit in a strange livingroom in front of a TV set for three hours. Or the time his father dropped him off to go fishing and picked him up six hours later starving and freezing. Or the many times he has called, inviting him to the movies, and then never shown up.

Too bad this isn't fiction. It's sad to think of parent child relationships which are so poor. But they exist. What happens to a kid when he's raised on broken promises? It's underneath such treatment where the real damage lies, for little by little, the child begins to feel that he's undeserving and not important enough to matter. It's a terrible kind of shattered trust that goes on to wound deeply, and sometimes mortally, the child's concept of his essential worth.

I learned how essential trust is in the parent-child relationship in an unusual and public way. The occasion was that August 1973 Christian Family Movement Conference at Notre Dame when the Bosco family—as a family—was leading the workshops on Single Parent Families, hoping to show by our presence that one-parent families did not have to consider themselves "broken", that they could be whole, complete, and loving families.

During one of the sessions, after a long, lively dialogue mostly between the participants and my children, one woman said to my daughter, Mary, "You seem to have such a good relationship with your mother. What do you think accounts for that?"

Mary thought a moment and then said, "Trust. She always trusted us even when we didn't deserve it. What I mean by that is she never gave up on us or made us feel unworthy. She would say, 'You did a *bad thing,* my *good Mary'.''*

It was one of those moments when you swallow hard and hold back the joyful tears. A moment of revelation. Trust—the assurance a child has that he/she can depend on you. It is a beautiful thing. With it, there's a mutual, growing sense of connection between you as the child weans away from you into adulthood. Without it, there's an invisible shield which may allow for a surface, cold politeness between you, but no possibility of touching.

Shortly after Christmas, I stopped by one evening to see Pat for a few minutes. Coincidentally, Bobby's father called that same evening to ask him, "Would you like to go to the movies?"

"No thanks," he answered. *I don't want to go.*"

These were loaded words—rejection, the boy's survival kit. It was the beginning of the end, but I'd place bets that his father never caught the message.

In my 27 years of parenthood, I have become convinced that the absolute basic connection between parent and child is trust—that strong, strong quality of being able to be consistent, honest, fair and living-in-love with children. With trust present, the family is solid and blessed. Without it, the delicate balance is shattered and the home is broken.

What is trust? It is a promise that will not be broken; an assurance that you will never turn your back and walk away from the person you claim to love; the confidence that your love is unconditional, not subject to if's, but's and exceptions; the communication of yourself as one who has wisdom, is in equilibrium internally and externally, and consistently treats loved ones with care. Trust is home base—that place of refreshment, light and peace where all the world is a benediction—with a new insight: the recognition that "place" was always a "person", being in the presence of one who loves you.

Before birth, trust is automatic. The growing infant is encapsulated in security, with all his needs and comforts satisfied by his benevolent, circular world, which has no angles, no sharp points, no adventurous unknowns, no threatening horizens. But when the child's head begins to bang against the closed door and he demands that the birth process begin, the old trust is left behind and a new one must begin.

In a book charmingly called, *What Do You Say to A Child When You Meet A Flower?* (Abbey Press), the psychologist author David O'Neill, writes:

"It seems that quite early in the child's life he becomes conscious that there are good and bad things around him. There are things to reach out to and things to be afraid of. He is not always right in judging which is which, but his instinct is very right in helping him sense that total love is what he needs. He expects his parents to provide this. So he casts his mother and father as hero and heroine in his drama of life . . .

"The baby lives in the same real world as we do and can never be completely sheltered from its problems. He is very vulnerable in this strange world. He can grow to deal with it, only if he is secure in love. *When this happens, he is able to trust his world.* The difficulties and the problems, the pains and the aches and the anxiety do not disappear. He finds something bigger than all these. He finds love and enters into trust.

"Trust is about the biggest thing that will happen to him during his first five or six years. Nothing else will be so important. It is the shape which responsive love takes in a growing child. It is a response to the steady, unchanging love he senses in his mother and father. It is the center-point of his world. Whenever anything looks like it's going wrong, he turns back to this center."

Because trust provides the security-base from which a child reaches out to life and the world, it must be nourished with care. The trust given or not given by parents will determine markedly the attitude towards people and the world that children will carry with them throughout their lifetimes.

This is a frightening realization for single parents. It means that in all our work to provide home, food, clothing, an education and more for our children, it will all be sounding brass and tinkling symbols if we fail to put all of this giving, all of this interaction on a rock-solid platform of trust. This is a heavy problem for us, because, as I've said before, our children have experienced death—the death of a parent or a relationship—and death is the ultimate betrayer of trust.

"Everytime I go out of the house, my four-year-old starts screaming. She remembers her daddy went out and never came back and she thinks I'm going to do the same," complained a young widow.

Another woman told how her young adolescent daughter developed a tremendously withdrawn personality because of severe anxieties suffered after her parent's divorce.

"She had this constant fear that something terrible was going to happen, that I wasn't going to be strong enough to make it, raising my three children alone. She had this horrible vision of me collapsing and dragging my children down with me."

Little by little, as the young girl began to see that day after day her mother remained strong, was home each evening to talk with the children, help them, listen to their problems, the anxieties began to fade and she was able to trust again in her mother.

That is, of course, how trust is generated, recognized and accepted—through experience. No parent can talk a child into trusting him or her. It is not a negotiable commodity. It is a quality of a relationship, born out of the relationship itself.

I remember a so-called joke which I always detested, but which makes a great point about trust. There was this father who told his son that he was going to give him an important lesson. "Go up on the roof," he said. When the boy was on the roof, he looked down. His father was standing there, with his arms stretched, saying, "O.K., now jump."

The boy hesitated and the father cajoled him," Come on, jump. I'm your father, you can trust me."

As the boy jumped, the father stepped back. Later, in the hospital, full of broken, plaster-casted bones, the boy said, "Dad, why did you do that? I trusted you."

The father answered, "That's the best lesson you'll ever learn, you fool. Never trust anyone."

More parents than we'd like to believe are like that father—betraying their child's trust, changing their promises. The broken bones of the story are only symbolical of the broken hearts, placed in plaster casts for life by children who learn that this hardness is the only way to protect themselves from further vulnerability and pain.

I knew one young woman, living with her mother who was on a very low income and who nourished a dream of going to college on her father's promise that he would "take care of her education." When it came time for her to apply, he suddenly changed his mind.

"I'm getting married again," he told her, "and I'll need all my money."

Eventually, she worked her way through business school, but she carries a burden. "I'm never going to have children," she said. "I wouldn't want to take the chance of being the same kind of parent my father was to me."

That's only one example of how fragile trust can be. Sadly, parents are often unaware of the various factors in their relationship with children which work against the development of trust.

I have compiled a list which I call the "devious dozen"—the twelve major, but unsuspected, blocks which trip up trust between parents and children: 1) conditional love; 2) judgmental attitudes; 3) inconsistency; 4) can't be pleased parent; 5) impatient parent; 6) conflicting personalities; 7) conflicting choices; 8) parental indifference; 9) touch-me-not parents; 10) perfection-oriented parents; 11) self-centered parents; and 12) negative carry-overs from parent's own childhood.

Let's look at a few of these and how they have special implications for single parent families.

Conditional love is devastating. The child literally has to *earn* his or her parents' love. If the child studies hard and gets good grades, his father will pat him on the back. If he cleans his room, he gets a hug from mother; if not, a spanking. If he does this . . . he can go to a ball game. If he doesn't . . . punishment for offending his parents. If he stops performing well . . . he gets a lecture.

In single-parent families, a mother or father can place conditions on love almost without being aware of it. Just by being in a position where life is tough, where partnership is gone, where burdens are unshared, puts you in danger of expecting, unfairly, that your children should automatically and without instruction, take over some of your burdens. If the child makes life easier for you, then you love the child. If he doesn't, or actually makes life harder, you withdraw your love.

Conditional love also lays a guilt trip on children. If a child begins to resent the intrusion into his time, his personality, his hobbies, his own plans, he runs the risk of feeling unhappy, cruddy, selfish. He's well into guilt, the self turned hangman.

Worst of all, conditional love sets a child up as a love-seeker always looking for love in the wrong places, using the wrong methods. I knew a woman who knocked herself out for everybody. She was the neighborhood free babysitter; the neighborhood chauffeur; the block volunteer for collecting for every disease known to mankind; the worker in every church affair. One day she went to a psychiatrist for help because she began to suspect that her dedication to serve strangers was not normal. The psychiatrist had her talk about her childhood. She was the oldest child in a single parent family who came home from school every day and diligently took over her mother's chores. When she was working, her mother smiled. If she wanted to go to a movie, her mother would sadly go on about how could she be such a selfish daughter, thinking only of her pleasure while her mother was home, slaving. The case was classic. She had to earn love as a child; the pattern was set; she was still trying to earn "love."

A child who has to earn love, always standing under the threat of having love taken away if he fails in performance, becomes a person with distorted attitudes about the very meaning of life itself. He is not valued in himself, for his very sharing of the gift of life. His value comes out of his productivity and servitude. Thus, his expectations always stay on the debased level where all relationships stand when defined in terms of buying and selling.

Judgmental attitudes of a parent also shape the child/parent relationship negatively if the judgments focus on the child instead of on the behavior. Using any terms like naughty, bad, disgraceful, to describe a child says to the child, how can my parent love me when I am that terrible person?

Single parents are particularly vulnerable to being judgmental because we see ourselves as being in a position of being judged and subconsciously can turn this focus around, placing it on our children. As parents alone, we feel society looking at us, amost challenging us to fail so it can be proven right about its negative attitudes towards our families. It becomes terribly important to us to show the world that we're o.k., our children are o.k., our families are o.k. This uptightness can harm us, particularly if it becomes unreasonably unbending about our children's behavior, judging faults and even minor actions as a threat to the solidity we're trying to achieve. Our fear is that if our shades are pulled down, we'll be bared and subject to societal scrutiny and judgment.

Therefore we are liable to become super cops over the children, calling them, and not their actions, bad if they misbehave. *Bad* children know they can't be trusted and so the judgment erodes the essential relationship.

Inconsistency is another great way to keep a child off-balance, insecure and unsure of a parent's love. I met a single mother recently who oohed and aahed, hugged and kissed her three-year-old for bringing her a bouquet of dandelions. The next day, the child picked some tulips from the flower bed, and the mother screamed, ranted, raved and spanked her for her destructiveness. That was one confused three-year-old. The mother never saw anything wrong with her reaction, though she did admit that along with single motherhood, she had fluctuating moods of highs and lows.

Ups and downs are part of the inheritance which comes with single parenthood, particularly in the early months. You have all the classic disturbance conditions—identity crisis, low self-image, agression-regression, instant hostilities—the yo-yo syndrome. Can you imagine what it's like for the children to have to deal with a yo-yo parent? They can take it for awhile, and for a longer while if you do a lot of sensible laughing in between the ups and downs. But the distance between a slap one minute and a kiss the next is further than we can imagine in dealing with the delicate rooting of trust.

Some parents are so hard to please that the old expression, "even Our Lady's Juggler couldn't please them," would hold true. A student in one of my religion classes a few years back told me that while her mother had gone to the hospital for two days, for minor surgery, she had cleaned the house beautifully, even waxing the floors. When her mother came home, she walked through the house, examining the cleaning job, her usual habit. When she reached the door of the hallway closet, she ran her finger over one of the wood grooves, silently showing her daughter the dust on her finger.

"She never said thanks for anything I did. Probably because nothing I did ever pleased her enough," the girl told me. The day after she graduated from high school, she left home.

A danger that both single and couple-parents fall into is to become "perfectionists" in their expectation of what their children should accomplish. This results from the subconscious attitude that one's parental success—or failure—is determined by how the children turn out. I see this as a kind of cannibalism of children. No matter how important it is for single parents to think of ourselves a "successful", nothing rates in importance to the right of our children to wear their own successes and accomplishments, or failures, independently. If we communicate to them that they *must* achieve, for our sakes more than their own, we have put the relationship, again, on a buy and sell level, placing a price on something that is priceless and destroying trust.

Some parents get tired of raising children. They become impatient to have them grow up and get out. That's not too hard to understand, but parents should be sensitive to how easily a child can misunderstand their general fatigue as a particular lack of love for the children.

Again, this is a subtle and serious trap for the single parent. Our complaints about the tough life can be misunderstood, read by our children as weary, faded love. I remember once repeating to a friend what my doctor said to me when I became pregnant with my sixth child. I was depressed from being very much aware that my marriage was close to termination and that I would be raising my children alone. My doctor said, "Do you realize this pregnancy is setting you back five years," referring to the fact that my youngest was then five, starting school, and I could have been free to work and care well for the five children I already had. A new baby would now vastly complicate my life.

I had not realized that my son Peter, then about eight, was in hearing distance when I told this story. Later, he commented, "I made your life hard, didn't I? I'll try to grow up fast."

I started singing, "He ain't heavy, he's my son," told him he was a rotten kid to make my life so hard, that to make up for it, he'd have to bring me coffee and slippers . . . and silently vowed from then on to be "of love, a little more careful than of anything else."

Personality conflicts also abound between parents and children. Most parents never want to admit that it's easier to get along with some of our children than with others. I like to read quietly. It's much easier for me to live with my youngest son who also likes quiet hobbies than it was for me to live with my second son who liked barbells, rock music and motorcycles. Where trouble sets in is when a parent can't bend, says no to a child's expression of his own personality, or dominates the child by the expression of the parent's own. "Do it my way" is a most devastating parental rule, saying loud and clear, I don't trust you enough to let you develop according to your own personality.

Personality conflicts are easier to deal with in single-parent families because the child is bouncing off only one parental personality, not two. But difficulties erupt because a single parent very often has to struggle with lessened tolerance for family static. Because of this lower threshold of tolerance, personality differences, which of necessity manifest themselves in the daily action—or inaction—of the household, tend to take on more importance than they should.

For example, I'm a morning person, but three of my children are night people. They do their best school work and guitar practice at midnight. I'm a high energy person, zooming at chores, telling by actions that I really believe everything should have been done yesterday. Three of my children think everything can wait till the day after tomorrow. Without tolerance, simple things like a son's procrastination over taking out the garbage or cutting the lawn, can become the straw breaking the camel's back.

That's when, as a parent, you have to examine your values and your personality carefully, making sure that you distinguish between intolerance caused by a lack of concern for your values, and intolerance which is due to simple personality conflict. The one is very important; the second needs a mutuality of consideration. If we as parents don't distinguish the important from the less important, that's a shame, because our children surely shall.

In a single-parent family situation, parental attitudes about responsibility also impact seriously on the trust relationship. Can you imagine a non-custodial father inviting a child on a vacation to Disneyworld and then backing out? Can you further imagine this father going on that same vacation with a woman friend and sending his child a card saying, "Thinking of you!" That's a true story.

When a parent like that one has no concept of what responsibility means, the full burden falls on the remaining parent to nurture a child's badly damaged sense of trust. This isn't easy, because guidelines for what constitutes responsibility and what constitutes parental exploitation and/or downright martyrdom have to be tailor-made for each situation. If a four-year-old throws a temper tantrum because her custodial parent goes out for an evening, should the parent stay home? If a teenager knocks on her mother's door at two a.m., needing to talk out a problem, should the mother say, I need my rest to work tomorrow, or should she listen?

Responsibility has been defined by some simply by adding an "a" and a hyphen: response-ability. The single parent has to acquire enough wisdom to be able to analyze the child's need and to pray for the ability to be able to respond well. While we're praying, we'd better ask for stamina, too, because responsibility stays with us till they're grown. It's a pain, with immeasurable rewards, the greatest of these being trust between you because your love comes across as a permanent and sure thing.

Someone said once, "It's not enough to love your children. They have to *know* you love them." It's called getting the message across. If we don't communicate that love on a feeling basis, as well as on a reason-scale, trust can't happen.

Trust is generated when children literally breathe in love that is consistent and tender; when approval and disapproval are never dangled over their heads signalling a parental applause meter to go on and off; when they are allowed the freedom to test themselves and us, to make mistakes, to fall and to fail, without running the risk of losing us, too.

Trust means loving them enough to let them grow at their own speed, gently directed by us, grounded in the security of us. Trust is a surrender which demands that we love our children more than ourselves. It is the most difficult "yes" a parent will ever say.

Chapter 6
The Ultimate Goal-
Wholeness

Entry into single parenthood put me unexpectedly on a soapbox, made me an advocate of a cause, and researcher of a phenomenon. I became determined to change what I felt to be the most destructive problem facing the single parent—the societal image which labelled single-parent families "broken" simply because one parent was missing. I was particularly bothered because the very word "broken" implied that we were problem families, all experiencing behavioral difficulties with our children. I was convinced that *good parenting* is what children need and that this can be done by a parent alone. What's more, there was now and always had been plenty of evidence to prove that children raised by one parent also turned out to be well adjusted and productive adults.

I gave talks saying, "I want my family to be defined by its essence, by the atmosphere which permeates it, by the reality of the relationships of the members. It cannot be labelled simply by its external structure."

I wrote in an article: "One-parent families are different, but they are 'broken' only if they are disunified, lacking in love and mutual support, uncomfortable and disruptive. A family in which there is a sense of unity, peace, comfort, mutual support, and the unquestionable presence of love, is whole, not broken—regardless of whether it is headed by one or two parents."

My platform generated positive responses, encouraging me to keep up my advocacy. One of the most touching letters came from a woman in Illinois, who wrote: "I can vividly remember overhearing two nuns talking about my sister and me—'They are such nice girls and do well in school even though they're from a broken family.' I recall being so ashamed. I didn't know my family was broken! My mother had somehow managed to convey a positive image of our family to us and it took. You seem to be doing the same. God bless you!"

A very few scoffed at me, telling me to get the rose-colored glasses off. Single parent families, they said, were deficient and nothing I said was going to change that truth.

Well, it has been 11 years now since I started my campaign to get single-parent families recognized as *different,* but *whole,* families. Most gratifying, I am now not alone in that contention. In the fall of 1974, *New York Times* reporter, Georgia Dullea, conversed with me by phone at length in researching a story she was doing on divorce. When her article came out in the December 3, 1974 issue of the *Times,* she began, "Almost no one says 'broken homes' any more. Now they are popularly called 'single-parent families' and they are a way of life for one American child in every seven . . ."

In 1976, a Washington study verified that the number of parents was not a significant factor in how the children turned out. The Research and Evaluation Division of the United States Department of Health, Education and Welfare reviewed the findings of 200 studies concerning the effect of missing parents. Their conclusions indicated that the breakdown of *family functions,* not the break-up of the family, is the major cause of behavior problems and the other disintegrations labelled "broken family."

In plain language, broken families result in households where family functions are weak and abandoned, and this unfortunate situation can happen whether there are two parents in the family or one.

Now that I have come through my initial campaign and feel confident that single-parent families will no longer be automatically equated with brokenness, I am moving along to focus on what I see emerging as an even greater, more crucial problem facing single parents and couple-parents alike—the need to put a value on *good parenting* as the prerequisite for restoring the wholeness of family.

Right now, today, in our country, the American family is showing alarming signs of falling apart as a functioning unit; and, at the risk of sounding flip, being a child in America, is actually hazardous to health. Look at a sampling of the signs:

• Family styles—other than single parent families—are emerging, with no attention or recognition being given to them as having a negative impact on solid family life. For example, what alterations happen in families headed by an unemployed father? How many new conflicted families are created by remarriage? How many are "dinner families", where both parents are gone from the home for work from eight to 10 hours a day or more? How many are disrupted families because of conflicts with teenagers over such issues as alcohol, drugs, open sex, fringe religious groups, the denigration of their traditional family and religious heritages?

• The chief cause of death for persons under 18 are accidents; and children lose a total of 15 million school days a year because of accidental injuries.

• The suicide rate for youth from ages 15 to 19 has more than tripled in the past 20 years, increasing from 2.3 per 100,000 in 1956 to 7.1 in 1974. Suicide is now the third leading cause of death among American youth.

• Child abuse by parents has reached an incredible two million battered child cases a year, resulting in the death of nearly 200,000.

• American crime has become a youth problem, with juvenile crimes increasing three times as fast as adult crimes. Almost two million youths under 18 were arrested for criminal acts last year.

Would good parenting prevent these horrendous statistics which indicate that so many of our youth are dallying with their own destruction? And if so, what has happened to good parenting—and why?

I can't answer that and I doubt if any authority exists that can. I have an opinion, however. I think good parenting has lost its status as a value in America today, supplanted by a frantic quest for adult freedom, individuality and the right to do *my thing, my way.*

Dr. Urie Bronfenbrenner, a noted child-raising expert from the College of Human Ecology at Cornell University, has described this shift and its implications for the future of the American family. He states:*

"That the family is the central institution comes as no surprise to most anthropologists, ethnic patriarchs, or social historians because the family is the only social institution that is present in every single village, tribe, people, or nation-state we know throughout history. But that the family is the core institution in every society may startle and annoy many contemporary Americans. For most of us it is *the individual* that is the chief social unit. We speak of the individual vs. the state, individual achievement, support for disadvantaged individuals, the rights of individuals, finding ourselves as individuals. It's always the individual, with 'the government' a weak second. The family is not currently a social unit we value or support . . . .

"It's transparent now that the family is a critically important institution in shaping our children's minds, values, and behavior. But it's equally clear that the American family is disintegrating. That's what I'd call a collision course for our society."

Not long ago, I read about a poster that had been put up in a Washington toy store making this commentary on American child rearing:

1910's: Spank them.
1920's: Deprive them.
1930's: Ignore them.
1940's: Reason with them.
1950's: Love them.
1960's: Spank them lovingly.
1970's: To hell with them.

*Quoted with permission from *Search,* State University of New York, 99 Washington Ave., Albany, N.Y. 12246, Fall, 1976.

Syndicated columnist, Dr. Saul Kapel, commented on this, saying, "More and more people say by their actions that they would rather have fun than children."

Within the past, year, I have read innumerable articles and surveys pointing out that for many Americans today, parenting is about as popular as having a case of measles—the birth rate is going, and staying, down; more and more child-bearing couples have decided not to have children, following the leadership of NON, a formal organization of couples dedicated to non-breeding of children; and a wave of "parental regret" has hit the country, with parents stating that if they had to do it over again, they would remain childless.

The first place I read about this discovery of parental regret was in a fall issue of *McCall's* magazine. They had Gallup do a survey for them and published the results, showing that 5.5 million parents of children under 18 would not want children again. The two largest groups of negative voters were parents between the ages of 18 and 29 and those over 50.

Reasons given varied from "too expensive" and "too much responsibility" to "the uncertainty of the world", "limitation of personal freedom" and "too much hard work." Interestingly, only one person in the sampling said that children were a disappointment.

The next place where I saw this subject come up was in an Ann Landers column, the most popular advice column in the country. Ms. Landers had put a question to her readers, asking, "If you had to do it over again, would you have children?"

Her report on the results started out, "Well, dear friends, the responses were staggering. Much to my surprise, 70 percent of those who responded said 'no'."

Calling the results the "most fascinating and disturbing" mail she had received in a long time, Ms. Landers published excerpts from some of the letters. One couple wrote, "We both agree our happiest years were before we had kids. They have brought us heartache and very little pleasure."

The *New York Daily News,* which has an Inquiring Photographer tapping New Yorkers on the shoulder, asking a daily question, also got on to the topic of parental regret, asking,

"Are children a blessing to parents in their old age?"

Answers were mixed. Interestingly, everyone who said yes, still qualified their answers with a but or however. As an example, "My daughter is a blessing. However, most children aren't a blessing to parents in the twilight of their lives."

The summary answer seemed to be, "no." When children are little, you have little headaches; when they are big, they become big headaches; and in your old age, who needs headaches?"

I have gone into this long discussion of the plight of the contemporary American family for a reason. Stated plainly, it is to turn on the alert siren and force us to face that the wholeness of families is being weakened by a parental attitude which has allowed the work and trouble of parenting to block out the worth and joy of it. We need to restore *good parenting* as a value.

Paradoxically, the one group today which has been examining the parental role, sometimes agonizingly, is single parents. We have been forced to think about our parenting and the nature of our family life. This concentration has come about out of our defensiveness from having been so long accused of being "broken," and out of our determination to succeed healed and healthy as a family after undergoing the trauma of alteration.

These factors, ironically, may in the long run make single-parent families the catalyst for restoring a concept, a value and a goal of wholeness for all American families.

Earlier in this chapter I explained what I see to be "wholeness" in the family. It is caring for each other and sharing so that a linkage results between the members, benefitting each, first with a sense of being loved, and then with the security that comes from this sense. Wholeness is the contradiction of isolation. It is the connection which brings order and sense into our lives. Wholeness is the only functional environment for our children's upbringing. Without it, children are brought down.

How does wholeness happen? Little by little, incident by incident, experience by experience.

Absolutely central to the concept of wholeness is the carrying out of family functions as a unity, with all members as participants. We've all heard the slogan, "The family that prays together, stays together." Well, that's a good start, but not the whole story. The family also has to eat together, work together, have fun together, be spontaneous together, be creative together, share its fears, its worries, its joys, its failures and successes. The caring has to be so strong that no hard lines are drawn. All the chores have to have fuzzy edges for easy crossover to help one another. I have hundreds of memories, each of which was a piece of the whole-ness.

When Frank was a high-school freshman, playing a role in West Side Story, the others did his house chores, freeing him to practice, so proud of their young brother. Paul couldn't type, so Mary breezed his term papers through the typewriter for him. Mary hated to cook, so Margy did it. Margy hated to iron, so Mary did that. Frank needed a cover for his amp, so Margy, our needle genius designed and made him one. John would get muscle strain from his wallpaper and paint job, so Frank would massage the ache out for him. Paul was the family math genius, tutor of them all.

One of my warmest memories is of Frank at age three, the blanket lover who guarded his security symbol like the treasure it was for him. Margaret, then five, was very sick with a fever, lying in bed. Frank, who wouldn't even surrender his blanket to the washing machine, brought it to her saying, "For you, Margy. My blanket will make you better."

That's family wholeness. It's also there in the spontaneity with which you throw some sandwiches together, herd everybody into the car and go to a park for a sudden picnic. It's also there when you have to admonish and punish. Margy and I remember, now with a laugh, the April day when I asked her to make supper and she replied, "No, I'm on vacation." It was the week after Easter and school was in recess.

I rarely raise my voice, but that day my reaction was loud enough to blow her off her tuffet, and she ran, not walked, to the kitchen to start supper. Sometimes you reason with them, but when they're unreasonable, you don't mess around about who's boss.

Family wholeness grows out of a total design which includes not only warmth, lovingness and security, but also is ordered and, above all, honest, if the mosaic is finally going to form a pattern. No family can be whole if individual members slack off and start to exploit the others, expecting to get away with having to make their particular contribution.

Single parents have to be on guard for the special problems that can splinter wholeness in our families. One is what I call the "Little Red Hen Trap." You remember the story, don't you, about the long suffering little red hen, who asked for help and only got excuses—so she planted the seed, tended the crop, harvested the wheat, ground it to flour and baked the bread. When it came time to eat the bread, she had a crowd in the house, all ready to grab, now that the work was done.

Single parents, in our desire to be both mother and father to our children, can easily fall into the trap of being successful overachievers. A family with a "little red hen" parent is not a functioning unit. It is a service station, with a serving martyr-parent becoming the feeding source and children becoming the takers, learning the constant lesson of becoming ever more selfish. The red hen parent confuses good parenting with uninterrupted servitude and ends up with a disintegrated family

Another cause of disruption in single-parent families, common in separated and divorced situations, results from a stormy or antagonistic relationship with the non-custodial spouse. I've seen families where parents keep forcing each other back and forth to the courts, fighting for custody of the children because it's in the best financial interest of each to keep the children. The children usually are emotional messes in these cases, living in the midst of continuous and bitter conflict.

In one family, a mother of three teenagers left her husband and children to set up housekeeping with a married man planning to leave his family. Her children all started evidencing behavior problems. She would visit them unexpectedly, sometimes for a few days at a time, and then leave again. While she was home, the children behaved better. When she left after these visits, they were in worse shape than before. The father was in the dilemma of trying to hold the family together while trying to control his anger. He threatened to kill his wife, adding to his children's disrupted family life. That is a broken family, as well as a broken marriage.

Women I have met at gatherings of Divorced and Separated Catholics relate how their ex-husbands refuse to comply with regular visiting schedules, but instead show up whenever they feel like seeing the children. Admittedly, trying to put one's house in order is difficult when visits from an ex-spouse are unexpected and unplanned. But often, the custodial mother is overreacting to what she assesses to be the negative effect of the father on the family. She becomes so lost in the emotional anger having her ex-spouse still act as if he has some rights over her and her domain, that she is unable to negotiate some kind of mutual agreement over how he can remain a functioning father above and beyond visiting rights contained in the separation and divorce agreements.

I have always maintained that, like it or not, a divorced mother must accept the fact that her ex-spouse will remain a part of her life at least until the children become adults. He, as parent, has a right to an association with his children; and they, his children, have a right to their parentage, father as well as mother. A single mother who fights father contact must make certain she has sound reasons for keeping children and their father separated. If the children themselves want this greater contact with the father, then this is a most compelling reason for mother compliance.

MOMMA, the California-originated organization for single mothers, faces this problem of parenting after separation and divorce not by bickering, but by re-education. They are working to learn problem-solving methods specific to their new child-rearing situations. One of their goals has been to set up "mediation centers", where ex-spouses can "put out on the table their own feelings of betrayal and despair and anger."

A spokesman explained, "We'd like to get over that terrible discounting—acting like you can't trust kids for one day with someone you lived with for 10 years. No matter how we feel towards each other, we're still Mom and Dad to our kids."

Wholeness in a family can't be had while wounds are unhealed, or worse, continually reopened. Until a mature and peaceful relationship—or absence—is worked out with the former spouse, the other parent of your children, the single custodial parent will have a most difficult struggle trying to achieve a united, solid, secure and loving family.

Another factor which unsettles single-parent families is the potentially transitory nature of the new family. Statistics indicate that 50 percent of single parents remarry and evolve new nuclear families within five years of their becoming single parents. These new families, involving often the merger of children from two different sets of parents, bring their own new advantages and problems. It is a fact, unfortunately, that remarriage often enough disrupts a family, unsettling the children all over again, shaking the wholeness.

I have often been asked why I never married again. First I joke and say because I haven't been able to choose from that long line of suiters waiting to be number seven in my life. But then I get serious and tell the truth. I have never considered remarriage because I have worked too hard to gain peace and unity in my family. If I remarry, I would introduce another personality, or personalities (if the man had his own children) into our lives and I'd be gambling that it would all work out fine. Gamblers lose more often than they win. I'm not saying my way is the right way for anyone else. But it is the only way for me, given the value-priorities I have chosen. I have no value that rates higher than the wholeness of my family.

Good parenting and a whole family have to spring from a vision. What is your vision of a child? Is it positive and clear enough to motivate you to take on the tough obligation of raising them with loving care, a job which exhausts you, eats up your income and takes away your freedom?

Good parenting is hard, hard work with no guaranteed prizes and, I admit, I have often wished it were easier. But it does have meaning. I get overwhelemed by all the beauty, intelligence, creativity and love that I see radiating out of my children, and that puts all the negatives into perspective.

Good parenting is our contribution to the continuation of life itself and the best training program for really understanding that it is only love which makes sense out of our lives. Because I am a parent, when I go to bed at night, I don't have to wonder, what did I work for today? It wasn't for a car, a house or a vacation. I worked for *life*, and for a unity, a joyful connection that is a whole family. Speaking strictly for myself, I wouldn't want to settle for spending my days on anything less important than life itself and the environment of wholeness in which life best thrives.

Chapter 7
Plugging into
Surrounding "Communities"

Several years ago, a sociologist named Jane K. Burgess did a study which she called "The Single Parent Family: A Social and Sociological Problem." Her findings, reported in the Journal of the National Council on Family Relations (Fall, 1970) paralleled very well the experiences which I and most of the single parents I knew were facing. She was especially critical of the "social vacuum" inherited by single parents. She wrote:

"Whatever the problem, families that have gone through a major disruption need help from members of the community. It is no time to desert them. The challenge to society is to develop institutions and values that will help the single-parent family live within the context of the whole family.

"We must not regard the single parent as different," she said. "It is a family in its own right."

In a low key way, Professor Burgess spelled out her challenge to communities to take a responsibility in helping single-parent families become de-isolated socially. She mentioned specific areas where communities could help our families establish new social roles. These included setting up such services as family counselling; financial advice; help in keeping a single parent home in repair; better day care opportunities; fathers inviting fatherless children into their social circle; church activities that encourage participation of single-parent families.

"It is this sort of encouragement and emotional support that the single spouse needs to restore her self-confidence and self-esteem as a person, and as an adequate parent," she wrote, adding:

"It also gives single parents the opportunity to expose their children to two-parent families so that they can grow up with a vision of a good marriage with husband and wife and children for themselves some day."

My personal belief is that the two crucial "communities" needing to activate a real concern for single-parent families are school and church. In an earlier chapter, I mentioned some of the school attitudes I had found particularly distressing. Since children spend so much of their day in school, and since school is for education—which is about the formation of a child's knowledge, attitudes and approaches towards life, development of potential and subconscious determination of values—we simply cannot underestimate the importance of the school experience in our children's lives.

Educators are finally getting around to noticing that out of a class of 25 students, anywhere from two to 10, depending on the income and ethnic mix of the school population, will be children living with a single parent.

An article in the Nov./Dec. 1975 issue of *Today's Education* stated: "The school and home life of a child cannot be independent of each other." I absolutely concur.

The authors further stated, "Teachers would be well advised to avoid stereotyping fatherless or motherless children as disturbed and in need of special attention." I concur again.

In actual fact, children's reactions to living in a one-parent family are as varied as the circumstances under which the maternal or paternal deprivation takes place. I would never deny that the loss of a parent can have an adverse effect on some children, making them hostile, agressive, disobedient and generally difficult to manage in a classroom situation. In these cases, teachers can be victimized, expected to do a good teaching job under an impossible setting of disruption. Schools should provide good counselling and proper outlets for helping trouble-making students and their teachers. The single parents of these hard-to-handle children need help, not criticism, from the school.

"When teachers receive the support they need to deal with children with problems, they may begin to hope for other programs to help these youngsters, such as a parent education program. Night courses in child rearing and child development could be made available to parents, giving them a chance to express their worries and anxieties about raising a child. This would be particularly important to the single parent. Hopefully, with school system support, single parents won't have to go it alone and neither will teachers," state the authors of "The One-Parent Child And The Classroom Teacher" *(Today's Education,* Nov./Dec. 1975).

One certain step that could be taken by schools is to see to it that all activities involving parents stress the *parent,* and not *mother* or *father.* In the summer of 1976, the Office of Civil Rights of the Department of Health, Education and Welfare ruled that father-son, mother-daughter events in public schools violate civil rights laws against sex discrimination and should be banned.

Gerald Ford, then our president, had an immediate "angry" reaction to the ruling, according to newspaper reports at that time, and hastily ordered the ban suspended. His press secretary, Ron Nessen, was quoted as saying, in explanation, "This is counter to the kind of traditional American values that he believes in."

The incident hit me personally. I had become very opposed to mother-daughter, father-son school events, but my reasons had nothing to do with "sexual bias." My concern had been for the sons and daughters who are left out of these school events because they don't have a participating mother or father.

Since I am a syndicated columnist for the National Catholic News Service in Washington, I expressed my feelings in a column, saying, in part:

"How do you think a boy feels when his friend asks if he's

going to the father-son basketball dinner and he has to reply, 'I don't have a father.' Or what about the motherless girl whose friend tells her, 'Too bad you can't go to the mother-daughter tea?'

"These used to be rare cases, and I suppose school officials could rationalize that since only a very few children would be left out in the cold, father-son, mother-daughter activities were justified. I would hardly put these into the category of 'traditional American values', however. Today, with some 27 million of the nation's children under age 18 growing up in fatherless or motherless homes, limiting school events to mothers-only or fathers-only is a 'tradition' which should be reevaluated, in fairness to the large numbers of children affected.

"I've seen first-hand how children react to being shut out of these special admission school events. They build defenses against their hurt. The easiest 'out' for them is to pretend that such events are a bore and that even if they did have a father or mother, they would have to be dragged kicking and screaming to such an uncool activity.

"What's especially sad is that fatherless or motherless children who are already living a deprivation are put in a position by their schools of having to face still another deprivation by being denied participation in these programs. No matter how good, loving, entertaining, and providing the solo parent is, the fact remains that the child's life carries with it a blank space that never goes away when one parent is missing. . . .

"There is a solution, of course. It is so obvious that I'm almost embarrassed to spell it out. Why can't school affairs be for parent and child—period. That would eliminate any aura of sexism and would put all children on an equal footing. If this simple request is trampling on a 'traditional American value', then I can only suggest that in the interest of fairness and justice to one in six of our American youth—the children of single parents—we scrap that 'value'."

Naturally, this column generated response. One letter from a father of five expressed very well the attitudinal problems still facing single-parent families. He did not really comment on the column, but used this as the springboard for attacking single parents who are divorced.

"Why is it," he asked, "that when divorced parents run into situations that do not fit their particular situation they always scream discrimination? In 75 percent of divorce cases, I honestly believe it is the self-centered, selfish desires of one or the other parent that is the cause of it.

"Women are constantly being prodded into self-fulfillment. The family doesn't come first. Her career or fulfillment does. Men are not without blame, as their careers are so demanding they have no time for wife or family. Now this is all their own business and personally, outside of times of concern for society, I don't give a damn. However, when divorced parents try to pass their own problems on to parents who stay together, I could vomit.

"You say these *victims* of divorced parents are loners and withdrawn because of society or a hundred other reasons. I wonder when any of you will admit, by God, it is one or both of *your* faults only . . .

"If I were married to a 'career woman', I seriously doubt if I could accept it. I have five children and my wife has enough work, recreation and volunteer jobs to fulfill her completely. I feel that if every man and woman took care of their own family and treated everyone else decently, we could put most of the social agencies out of business. If families worried about the spiritual and emotional development of their family as much as the material and pleasurable things, the problems would soon end.

"The mere thought that divorce is forced on most families by society is a sickening thought. I owe no divorced kid or parent any more than I owe my own family or another two parent family.

"I honestly feel a great amount of pity but not too much compassion for most divorced families.

> "Yours disgustedly,
> F. J. A.
> St. Louis, Mo."

Usually, I answer the many letters I get from my readers around the country. This was one of the few letters I did not answer, since it was so riddled with misquoted ideas and prejudices. But if I had, I might simply have said, "Welcome to the imperfect world, sir, and long before you, Cain also said, I am not my brother's keeper."

Attitudes such as this will plague single-parent families until communities accept us with love and not judgment. We, too, have a responsibility to communities to demonstrate by the way we live that we are not a weak and destructive element of society. But no matter what we achieve by way of solid family values, attitudes toward us will not be changed for the better until our accomplishments are recognized. It is gratifying to see beginning signs of this recognition among educators. I refer again to the authors of the article in *Today's Education,* who stated: "Many one-parent families are models of a close-knit unity which, in some cases, is a positive reaction to the one-parent situation."

The most logical community which could assist single parent families is the church, but from information I have been able to obtain, not much has been done by any religious denomination to give special attention to our families. Not long ago, I conducted a workshop on the special problems of Catholic one-parent families. The single parents attending— regardless of whether their singleness was caused by death, separation or divorce—expressed sadness and frustration over the disturbing reality that no program, no activities, no efforts geared to meet their many and complicated needs existed in their parishes.

It has only been in the past two to three years that single-parent families were even noticed by their churches. Just about three years ago, I received a call from a long-time friend who coordinates a religious education program for a parish of close to 3500 families. They had just finished doing an informal census in the parish to get a data-profile of the individuals and families which they felt would be a useful tool in helping them set up new programs for the coming year.

But a funny thing happened on the way to the countdown. With uncomfortable regularity, families kept cropping up with a missing dimension—a parent. By the time the census results were calculated, the workers had discovered that nearly 30 percent of the families in the parish were headed by a parent alone. Joan called me to ask if I would be willing to lead a program, give a talk, or do something that would let these families know they had been noticed. The parish leaders were frankly shocked. They hadn't realized that divorce, separation, death and abandonment had so infiltrated and changed the family-profile of a long-standing Catholic parish.

Since then, the word has gotten around that we exist in large numbers, but not much has been done besides giving a numerical recognition. Most churches have groups for teenagers, single adults, married couples, widows and widowers and senior citizens. But what support do they offer the parent alone who doesn't fit into any of these respected categories? Even more important, what support *should* they offer?

I would like to emphasize at this point that the neglect of single-parent families by churches has not been deliberate or conscious. The attitude has been more that there aren't very many such families and maybe the few that exist will just hide somewhere. I think we have been more an embarrassment than anything else. The Holy Family, the design for all Christian families, consists of father, mother and child. Too many sermons based on this image of the family and on the theological theory that perfect sacrifice in marriage makes all problems bearable, if not solveable, have caused a solidification of the definition of family. It doesn't allow for variation and, therefore, one-parent families are not being cast aside; they simply don't get easily recognized as Christian families.

Occasionally a case of outright judgment and rejection does happen. One woman, meeting with a group established for divorced and separated Catholics in my diocese related how she was asked by her pastor to resign as a religion teacher after her husband left her and obtained a divorce. The pastor put on a very kind face and told her he thought she'd be uncomfortable teaching in the religious education program when she herself had a "broken family!"

I believe the first responsibility the churches have is to recognize that single-parent families exist; that they are collectively stigmatized too often as "broken;" that this is unfair and warrants an all-out effort to create a positive image for such families. A diminished, negative image is still the heritage of single-parent families in their churches. Is there enough love in communities reflecting God's word—the churches—to change this?

In all the workshops I have conducted, a sincere desire to help and to accept help emerges on the part of both church representatives and single parents. The suggestion is often made that group sessions could be organized for single parents; this would enable them to get together to offer each other mutual support and consolation. One woman answered this suggestion very truthfully:

"But that doesn't solve any of my problems. When I come home from work, I'm exhausted, but I still have another job to do—housework, washing, transporting the kids to their activities, helping them with homework and so on. If I went out to a meeting, I'd only compound the guilt I feel at having to leave my kids all day to go to work."

I think the churches should experiment with real, practical programs for single parents, and these are a few of my suggestions.

A source of direct help to single-parent families could be a family-to-family outreach effort. This is how it worked in my case.

After the legal separation from my husband, I moved into a new neighborhood with my six children, then ranging in age from 16 down to two. My most pervading concern was Peter, the two-year-old, because I had to arrange full time care for him while I worked to support my children. As he grew older, the situation changed. He only needed part-time supervision, and it became increasingly difficult to find short-term baby sitting for the few hours elapsing between the time he got home from school and my arrival home from work.

Over the years, Peter had developed a very close friendship with a neighbor, Billy, and his family. Soon, they began "looking after" him when he got home from school and would have him play with Billy until I, or one of my older children, got home. That family had, and still has, my most sincere gratitude for giving me the best gift a single, working mother could have—peace of mind.

This family also took Peter on outings with Billy, to flea

markets, ball games and drive-in movies. They even took Peter with them on a trip to Niagara Falls. They have given Peter the love of a family. They are true Christian neighbors who have lightened my burden in a beautiful way and enriched my son's life.

I would caution that a family-to-family outreach effort should involve only the children. This will prevent any abuse of kindness; and it will eliminate any possible threat that a woman alone might be to another family. The relationship between my family and the family which has so often looked after Peter for me has been very successful because each family has always respected the privacy of the other. We never moved into each other's lives. Our contacts have been mainly an occasional phone call.

Another way that church families can help their single parent neighbors is to organize a church, or inter-church, Multi-Skills Bank. In every church population there are men and women from teens to grandparents who have skills to offer another. If an organized plan could be set up to get "experts" from the church membership to volunteer a small amount of time per week or month to assist a parent alone, this would be a decided corporal work of mercy. The bank could include such volunteer skills as plumbing, carpentry, car repairs, moving a piece of furniture, tutoring, giving driving lessons to teens, teaching arts, crafts, cooking, etc., social work or psychological counselling, and so on.

The following example shows how valuable an inter-church Multi-Skills Bank could be. When my oldest son Paul had his permit to learn to drive, I found that I was too nervous to give him lessons. The father of a family I know from the *Teams of Our Lady,* simply volunteered to do the job for me. He and Paul made all their own time arrangements, and I wrote the gentleman a thank-you letter from my heart after Paul got his license.

Sometimes a single parent needs a plumber to do something as simple as putting in a faucet washer. A woman usually doesn't have the tools or the foggiest notion how to do this. She often doesn't have the money to hire a plumber, either. A volunteer from the Multi-Skills Bank could give her this service, a real act of Christian charity.

At one of the workshops I mentioned earlier, one mother was distraught because her 16-year-old son had started smoking marijuana and refused to communicate with her. Another woman was in a constant teary state from severe depression. Neither had money for professional counselling. To have such services available through an inter-churches Multi-Skills Bank would indeed be an example of the members of the faith communities caring for each other.

Again, the problem of time and fatigue plagues the single parent who has little opportunity to teach growing sons and daughters how to cook, sew, plant a garden, do model airplanes, fix broken furniture, etc.

The Multi-Skills Bank can help here, too. Older church members have turned out to be marvellous teachers of upper-elementary-school-age children. It is a gratifying experience to see neighbors becoming "grandparents" to father-deprived, or mother-deprived children, teaching them how to cook, sew, grow vegetables and flowers, repair a wooden table, play chess and so on.

Skills which teenagers could put into the bank are sports coaching, babysitting at discount rates, tutoring younger children and helping with lawn maintenance.

In the area of spiritual activities, First Communion days can become a problem for some children if too much emphasis is placed on mommy and daddy bringing the child to the altar. The daughter of a woman separated from her husband became very upset that most of her friends would have "mommies and daddies" receiving communion with them which she would have only "mommy." The mother commented, "I don't fit in any more. My children and I feel isolated and 'abnormal'."

Perhaps more emphasis could be placed on family groups—rather than on nuclear families—joining together to present their children at the altar for First Holy Communion. Single parent children would not then feel so "different" in a group situation.

The existence of one-parent families in church membership is no longer a fact hidden away, unadmitted or unaccepted. We exist and are a part of the faith communities. We need the support of other families and communities. Together, we should pool our thinking and imaginations to come up with ways of mutual assistance so that we can go beyond survival and into the fullness of *living.*

One final suggestion for helping to plug single-parent families into the many communities which comprise our social environment is to open Single Parent Clubs in cities and counties for informal evening gatherings. One model for such clubs has been set up by the Community Service Society of New York, and is called the Single Parent Project. Located at 22nd St. and Park Avenue, the Project is a storefront where single parents can come to get information about where to get the particular help they need. This may be housing, jobs, medical care, counselling, legal assistance, financial advice and such.

At least once a week, the Project becomes a club where single parents come, with their children if they so choose, to talk about what their lives are like, what they'd like them to be like, and asking support and advice on how to get by just a bit better.

The parents, 95 percent of whom are women, most of them holding low paying jobs and supporting their children, like the "drop in" informal arrangement, in contrast to organized group meetings which usually turn into another pressure, something else that the harried single parent "must" do.

Since the Project is located in the heart of the city, the parents who come "are the real working poor," according to Sue Jones, the Project Director, herself a single parent. In an interview reported in the *Daily News,* March 8, 1977, she stated:

"They're too proud to take a handout and so their lives are a never ending grind. Often they lose time at work and subsequently they're fired because they spend days in family court waiting for their cases to come up. Or they take time off to see their kids' teachers.

"This is the kind of thing we'd like to change—if there were a little more flexibility in the schools and courts, if they had evening hours maybe once or twice a week, it could really ease the strain on these single parents."

The emergence of Single Parent Clubs in cities and suburban areas could be of great assistance to our families and also provide us with a forum for planning strategies for recognition and acceptance in communities.

The fact remains that even though the growth rate of single parent families has increased by 31.4 percent in the last 10 years—almost three times the growth rate of two-parent families—society has not yet caught us with or responded in any effective way to the changing needs and services required by single-parent families.

For this reason, our struggle as we build a new kind of intact family is intensified by societal resistance to us both on unspecified general principles and in its institutions. When the word gets around that we are single parents not usually by choice, but by decision—born out of our love and acceptance of responsibility—maybe then the world will say welcome.

This chapter is a shout—but is anybody listening?

Part 2
Accent on Parent

Chapter 8
The Family V.I.P.-You

I had been waiting for weeks to hear from my lawyer and find out, finally, how the judge had ruled on my petition for separation. This interim period was a deadly time of tension between a man and a woman who were in mourning over the death of their marriage—he with hostility, and myself with sadness. Like most mothers, I expected the judge to decide that my husband would have to leave and that the children and I would remain in the house. I felt the security of having our home was worth the uncomfortable waiting-out of the separation appeal.

Yet, the daily situation was frightful and the children were becoming nervous and upset. When one of my sons, then age six, began wetting the bed, I called the psychiatrist we had seen several times for marriage counselling prior to coming to the decision to separate.

"I need help," I said, in desperation. "I can't continue like this? What can I do?"

The proverbial moment of silence greeted me on the other end of the phone, and then his big, brusque voice jolted me with—

"What the hell are you calling me for? What are *you* going to do about it?"

I felt rejected, devastated, betrayed, uncared for, adrift and angry. At that moment, I hated that man passionately. I had asked for help, and he had thrown me—where?

Within 10 minutes, I was in the car, my daughter Mary with me. We went to a rental agency and, shocking myself, I generated the courage to ask if they had a three-bedroom house for rent. Before the day was over, I had found a house. I called the movers that same day. Two days later we left the home where I had raised my children and moved into a rented hi-ranch in the next town. It was drastic and final. The waiting game was over. The disordered and destructive life was behind us. The new and terrifying life had begun.

The fear, however, was balanced with a new revelation about myself. *I* had done this. *I* had taken responsibility and acted. *I* had caused a change in our lives out of a conviction that this was the best decision for myself and my children. It was my giant step forward into being frighteningly on my own two feet. There I stood, not where someone else had placed me, but where I myself had chosen to be. We were finally away from the pathological environment of tension and hostility, because of my own action, my decision to risk a massive change and face the consequences, and my courage to give up the security of the house.

That first night in bed in a strange place, I thought about the phone call I had made a few days earlier to the psychiatrist. All the hatred I had felt for him had blown away in the activity of packing and moving. Now I had time to think about what he had done—and I blessed him.

He had bluntly forced me to understand and accept the new reality of my life—that no "father figure" would be there to make decisions for me; that no strong male would be around to make my life easier. He had told me in his own way that if I were going to make it, it would be because I took responsibility, as a mature adult, for making the decisions which would shape myself and my family from now on.

"Thank you, Dr. Riley," I said aloud.

The starting point for every single parent is the place I was at that night, recognizing that you are the Very Important

Person in this family, and that if you can accept the burden of taking responsibility for yourself, you're on the move for a good and maybe even better life.

Unfortunately, the road, we're on in making that move is full of pitfalls and obstacles.

The most serious of these blocks may be an overdose of unselfishness. The single parent, particularly if he/she is very family-focused, can plunge into the work responsibility and come up unbalanced. No one can be happy without asking, at least occasionally, "What do I want for myself?" Yet, some single parents ignore that question, until their family-centeredness backfires on them, manifest by uncomfortable feelings of hostility, boredom or depression. This condition is more common in older women than any other category of single parent, particularly in a woman who was trained religiously to believe that self-sacrifice for the comfort of others is a virtue.

I have known single mothers who never go to a hairdresser; wear old clothes; deprive themselves the luxury of going to a concert—all for the spoken reason, "I can't afford it." Yet, these same mothers find the money to send their daughters to a beauty parlor, buy new clothes for the children and purchase concert tickets for the teenagers.

Actually, I, myself, am one of these the-children-come-first mothers, but I'm improving. A few years ago, I hit the doldrums, a condition which happens periodically and forces you to look critically at your life. I had the strange vision of seeing myself as a personified feeding station. My nurturing role had become so primary that it had absorbed me. A strange restlessness shook me and I wavered between determination to ignore it and depression, with depression winning out.

Rather than face the truth that I was quietly screaming because I had, literally, blanked myself out, I put the focus on place instead of self. What was wrong with my life was my location, Long Island, particularly in February, I reasoned. It was a damp, bleak place to live, with congested roads, no opportunity for a decent social life for families like mine, and dull, dull, dull. I yearned to move to a place where there would be sun and warmth and maybe the opportunity for a new life along with a change of scenery.

At that very time, I happened to see a copy of *Arizona Highways* magazine, and that marked the beginning of what came to be known in the family as mom's Arizona Caper.

It began with a lot of fantasizing about how great it would be to head west and settle in a place completely different, even down to the foliage. Being the practical type, I supplemented my dreaming with reality, writing for all the information I could get about Tuscon and Phoenix, even subscribing to their daily newspapers. I also began applying for teaching positions.

Within two months, my research completed, I was ready to put my house up for sale and move. Common sense told me I should look the place over first, but where was I going to get $300 for a round trip ticket to check out Arizona?

The answer came in my mailbox. Absolutely shocked, I opened an envelope from Macmillan publishers in New York, finding a check for $332. The money was for royalties on two books, published by P. J. Kenedy and Sons back in 1960 and 1962, books that I believed had long been deceased. The letter of explanation said that Macmillan had bought the inventory from a publisher who had bought out Kenedy, then out of business, and these were my royalties from final closeout sales.

Obviously, the good Lord wanted me to take that trip to Arizona. I still had to wrestle with the guilt that I would be traveling by myself to a strange state, leaving my children alone for five days or so. Considering that their ages then began with 21, 19, 17, and down, it hardly made sense for me to worry about their capability of caring for themselves. I rationalized on my way to the ticket office that the trip was an essential pre-preparation segment to an important moving plan.

During the last week of April, I flew to Tuscon. In roughly about one hour after landing, I knew I would never be able to live in the somewhat desert setting. Within two hours, I was missing the ocean desperately. By nightfall, the dryness had attacked my sinuses badly. In the morning, I cancelled the interviews for a possible teaching position, and decided not to despair, but rather to try to make the best of a bad idea.

Battling my practicality, and thanks to a credit card, which I used only sparingly and never on a whim for myself, I rented an air-conditioned LTD and spent the next five days having a great time touring Arizona.

By the time I was back east, flying over New York at night, looking down at the gorgeous sky-high view of the lights and bridges—every bit like jewels and necklaces on black velvet—I was embracing my fate of being a New Yorker, reveling in the beauty of my place.

Remarkably, I came home emptied of my restlessness and depression, quite my old, enthusiastic self. Why should I have been "cured" when I didn't actually change anything in my life, or at least it so appeared?

Eventually, I understood. For the very first time in my life, I had done something I wanted to do, just for myself. I had spent money on me, had been away from children for the first time in 21 years, had travelled a far distance alone for the first time in my life. For a brief time, I had stopped being a feeding station and had briefly changed scenery. I had cared about myself and had given myself a gift—five days for me alone.

The effect was most therapeutic and educational, pointing out so clearly that every person needs to emerge regularly as an individual, taking a deserved share of the good life. It was a lesson and an experience I sorely needed then and have benefitted from ever since.

The story has a funny sequel. A week after I got back from Arizona, I got a letter from Macmillan telling me they had made a computer error on my royalty check. I was supposed to get $3.32 and would I please immediately return the $328.68 over payment. That's when I knew the trip had been just what I needed and had been arranged by a Wisdom greater than mine. Instead of getting depressed, I giggled like a kid. It took me six months to save the money and get it back to Macmillan, but where else could I have "borrowed" money, interest-free for a five-day excursion into revivification?

I tell this long story not to suggest all single parents should take a vacation in Arizona, but, rather, to point out a basic truth that we, in this position, are in danger of ignoring, fatally. Each of us has to care about ourselves as individuals. It is our honest and fair right to protect ourselves from being cannibalized by the demands of our responsibilities. Because of our situation, we are prime candidates for a range of quasi-pathological conditions if we allow ourselves to become a *function*—parent, nurturer, breadwinner, etc.—instead of the *person* in charge of those functions.

The most serious of these destructive reactions is depression, not an easily definable condition because it ranges from a simple form, like "having the blues" to a most serious state where medical treatment is needed. Depression is always a cry. It is deep and, translated with blunt simplicity, it says, "Look at me. Care about me. I'm a person, too." It is a condition which hits women hardest. "The ratio is two to one, and that's world-wide," writes psychiatrist Nathan S. Kline, author of *From Sad to Glad, Kline on Depression* (Putnam).

Reasons given by professionals for this high incidence of female depression fall primarily into a common denominator: Women become depressed when they feel they are not the ones directing the course of their own lives.

"Women are conditioned to play a passive, waiting role in our culture," stated Dr. Freyda Zell, a feminist psychologist, in a newspaper interview. "Women don't feel in control of their lives and turn their anger inward against themselves (depression). Women have to learn how to express anger openly."

Wanda Frank, a psychiatric nurse-professor from Downstate Medical Center in Brooklyn, interviewed for the same article, brought out the relationship between depression and social conditioning in single women. "Women are told they have no status without a man." She adds, "(Women) wouldn't feel depressed if they believed they had mastery over themselves and their environment."

Considering the fact that single mothers have "lost" a man; have usually "dead end" jobs, with virtually all their earnings going for family support; and have little opportunity to change their location of employment or house, few of us escape a rendezvous with "down in the dumps" days, or even severe depression.

Not too long ago, again after giving a talk at a workshop on Divorced and Separated Catholics, a woman came to me to ask my help. Within a few minutes, her eyes were teared. "I cry all the time," she said "I don't care about anything. I don't even think I want to live. My children would be better off without me."

She was obviously severely depressed, and I could empathize and share her suffering. I have only once in my life undergone *severe* depression, but it left me in mortal terror of ever being in such a state again and ever grateful to God that I came through it.

A book written by Percy Knauth (Harper and Row, 1975) tells of the author's long bout with depression and his eventual healing. What struck me was the title he chose for his book—*A Season in Hell.* Depression could not be more effectively defined. It is precisely "a season in hell."

It's not too hard to understand what depression is. When you get through all the various situations related by depressed people as causes, there's a bottom line which shows that depression is really a reaction to anger—but anger insufficiently expressed—so that the anger turns inward and goes underground, settling pathologically inside a person. It's not the loss of a job, death of a child, a divorce, growing old, and so on, which causes a person to become depressed, but, rather, the internal anger-reaction to these.

The resulting trauma is devastating. You become immobilized, unable to make decisions; uninterested, unable to care about anything; terrorized, because you are unable to communicate. The resulting isolation from not "connecting" with other human beings is an unbearable loneliness. You become a frustration to friends and relatives who alternately emphathize and criticize. They tell you to look up and see the sun and the trees. They don't know that for the person who has lost hope, there is no sun, there are no trees. To be immobilized, detached, terrorized, hopeless and isolated is to be in hell.

Even the poet Dante had that concept of hell. In his *Inferno,* he leads his readers through the dark regions of hell with this warning overhanging the entrance—"Abandon hope all ye who enter here." As he unfolds the stories of the tragic, doomed figures, you proceed with him deeper and deeper into the regions of hell, where sins become ever more heinous. Finally, when you go with him to the innermost center of hell—where Satan is—how do we find the Prince of Darkness?

He is immobilized—frozen—encased in ice, in eternal isolation—in *hell* . . .

Psychiatrists agree that if a person is going to conquer depression, it will be because he/she has been able to develop self-esteem and introduce new activities, changes, goals and the like, bringing hope, optimism and confidence back into their lives. It can be overcome. I know because I did it. I also know that the two most important occasions in my life which dissolved my depression were the move from my home, with my children, to get away from the old, destructive life and begin our new one together; and the trip to Arizona, which gave me back a sense of personal worth and individual self-value.

Another serious problem affecting one's sense of self as a single parent is the tendency to feel devalued. Are you really worth anything? Does it matter if you get up and face another day?

Single parents have told me that if it weren't for the fact that they are needed by their children, they would be hard-pressed to figure out what life meant.

·   This, too, is another anger reaction. It comes mainly, I believe, from a sense of betrayal. We expected to live our life in love and unity with another person. We were trained to think of marriage as the complete life; the single state was vocally approved, but defined denigratingly as "spinster-hood;" the religious life transcended both by being defined as a somehow mystical "marriage" with God. The key word was marriage—unity.

No wonder, then, when the marriage is over, we are left with a void, not only physical but emotional. It is a terrible void, a state of having no one with whom to share your life. We have a missing essential in our lives, one which a person raising a family desperately needs—intimacy with another person. Intimacy—that communication which is a total connection of two people, creating an energizing force which relaxes, enriches, and enobles them on all levels.

Single parents have lost that and have become disconnected. No wonder we can fall into the trap of feeling devalued. A severance is always loss.

Because of my divorced aloneness, I could write poetry about the beauty of marriage, when it really exists. I can think of no better way for human beings to live than in an intimate one-to-one relationship, growing together at the same rate of speed in the same direction, setting aside their apartness and separateness to bring a share of their essence to one another. When marriage is the reality of two people being drawn out of their aloneness into union, constantly working at loving, knowing and understanding each other, where could one find a better way to live?

The reality of my life is that I don't have this marriage. I have, however, myself, my self-respect, my children and their love. Somewhere, after my entry into single parenthood, I shifted the gears, redefined personal value and filled the void of losing a marriage by accepting the challenges, without regret, of adapting to the different highs and lows of single life. On the plus side, as a single, the road map is largely our own creation, becoming more so as our children grow older and responsibility lessens. The very unpredictability of the single life gives it verve; add the fact that decisions are ours to make about how to spend our free time as the focus on parenthood lessens, and the single life can well come up roses. I'm not there yet, but I'm on my way. The sense of loss will always be milling around me, and in nostalgic moments, I, like the rest of the human race, may cry a bit for "what might have been." The past, however, is over, and here I stand, alone, but important and knowing this.

We can never accept our own importance if we are carting around a poor self-image. This image thing is another pitfall on the new road of single parenting. Self image involves not only how we view ourselves, but also how others, like relatives, neighbors, parish, business, and so forth, regard us. In days past, the terms *divorced woman* and *working mother* came across like a shout that these are the two greatest menaces to society. That's changed now, except for a residue effect that lingers subconsciously. The failure image after a broken marriage is also lessened, but lingering. Negative images have no justification and single parents must reject these. There's an old saying that "we are treated the way we allow ourselves to be treated." Single parents must insist on being treated with new respect, not old prejudices.

We have to accept the fact that our self image is changed, but that doesn't mean for the worse. It can be a much improved self image over what we had in marriage, particularly when divorce is the cause of the marriage end. I've known of husbands who have told their wives, "I can't stand looking at you, you're such a slob, or you're so fat, or you're stupid." I knew a wife who wouldn't eat with her husband, telling him she thought he was disgusting at the table. What kind of self image can people have within such marriages?

We may no longer be the "respectable" married man or woman, but we are still good people, trying to live up to our responsibilities. The courage we show in trying to build new lives in spite of the very difficult situations we are in means we are actually people who are successfully solving our problems, instead of remaining frozen and immobilized in our problems. That deserves a good self-image.

Single parents must be on guard against falling prey to a condition which is every bit as serious as depression. This is self-pity, a most unproductive and destructive state of regression. I made this point once in a talk, and a woman in her early 50's stood up and gave me an argument. She had a right to feel sorry for herself, she said. She had given the best years of her life to a man who had walked out on her and she was not about to be consoled. Her neighbors, friends, relatives and "everybody", she said, knew how rotten she had been treated and told her it was a shame that this terrible thing had happened to her. The message she made perfectly clear was that she was determined to enjoy her misery.

How do you respond to that degree of single-mindedness? I told her that I still maintained self-pity was akin to sitting in a corner, sucking your thumb, unproductive, unhealthy and unattractive. However, if that's what she wanted to do, it was her choice. She'd have to accept that I refused to sprinkle holy water on that kind of inactivity. I hope she got jolted out of her corner.

The single parent who is likely to fall into self-pity is one who was used to getting a lot of support from the now-gone spouse; who was dependent; did not exercise self-determination; and made few decisions. The self-pity reaction causes grown people to see their problems resulting from someone else's actions. Dr. Gary Singleton, a psychiatrist from Georgetown University Medical School, said in a newspaper interview that putting blame on someone else is as old as our first parents, when Eve blamed the serpent for her downfall.

"Blaming others is built into the human race," he said, "but the more intensely you focus your life on others, at least in terms of gearing your life and reactions to others, the more you are likely to have a tendency to blame others when things get uptight."

The antidote for self-pity is just about the same as the cure for depression. If we can find an activity, a new interest, a hobby, a good work, a focus outside ourselves; accept responsibility for our own lives; develop self-reliance; meet new people; and begin to feel in control of our lives; then self-pity will be too far out of range to be even a threat.

One quality we must have if we are going to survive well as a person who also happens to be a single parent is assertiveness. This has been made a household word by the women's movement, and, unfortunately, has been misunderstood.

The very word, assertiveness, has a pushy sound to it, and that's too bad. I remember once being in a large department store where a woman was making a scene because the manager of the shoe section wouldn't take back a pair of shoes that looked as if they'd been worn for six months. A woman standing next to me lamented, "There's a bold one. She sure knows how to assert herself."

Like many people, she was confusing "assertive" with "loud and dishonest", and certainly implying that assertiveness was not a virtue. The incident pointed out how a good word can stir up bad vibes because of long-standing connotations. It would be a shame if using the word assertiveness to describe necessary growth-change in women backfires, continuing to be equated with boldness, or worse, agression.

Assertiveness, as I've come to see it, is vastly different from agression, which is a vice, and from impolite, demanding boldness, which is a character flaw. Assertiveness is positive and essential for well-balanced living, for it is your vote of confidence in yourself, demonstrating that you value your own judgment, rights and needs enough to speak up for these, without excuses or apologies.

If you're wondering whether any of this applies to you, just ask yourself, have you ever said yes to something which was not your responsibility or obligation, when you really wanted to say no? Have you allowed people to intrude upon your rights, your time, your energies, resenting it, yet not stopping it?

If I think hard enough, I could cite dozens of examples where over the past years I got myself into jobs and situations I wouldn't have chosen if I had been able to assert myself— being chairperson of a committee; attending meetings of no real interest or value to me; writing releases for various self-serving organizations; having lunch out when I'd rather eat a sandwich at my desk and read a book; allowing unexpected visitors to come in, feeding and entertaining them, while ignoring swollen legs and aching head. Most of this self-abuse was a carry over from past insecurities, reinforced by a marriage breakup, which made me afraid people wouldn't like me if I said no. No is a new language that I and most single parents, have to keep practicing, if we're ever going to achieve that essential control of our own lives.

Assertiveness is part of the "no" language. It means that you have learned to set your own standards for your behavior and that you choose to live by these, without apologies. It means putting an end to having others exploit you; respecting yourself; admitting honestly that your personal needs are just as important as the needs of others. For women who were raised to be submissive, ultra-polite, generous to the point of martyrdom, self-assertion is a tough new ball game. That's why Assertiveness Training has become a study in itself, attracting many women.

Assertiveness is, very simply, ourselves, getting to know our rights and needs and learning to express these. It results in a welcome change—replacing frustration with calm self-confidence.

No matter what distorted images the word assertion may

generate, when defined properly, assertiveness for single parents is an idea whose time has come.

Finally, the matter of our "identity" has to be faced. Without exception, every time I have conducted a workshop for single parents, some one or more bemoan the fact that they don't know who they are; that they are fed up with acting out "roles" imposed on them; that they want to be themselves; that they're undergoing an identity crisis.

To be perfectly honest, I don't know what it means to say "I want to be me." People talk about identity as if you can erect it like a monument, set it up and look at it. Identity has become an island—and that's a strange contradiction.

For identity has meaning only in relationship.

When I was in college, I remember being bored to yawns in Philosophy class when we had to discuss the famous question: If a tree falls in a forest, where there is no one around to hear it fall, does it make a sound? Or, for that matter, if a tree stands there, and no one is around to see it, is there a tree? Who cares? I thought. Of course there's a sound and a tree—scientific fact.

But as I became wiser, I realized the question was really a statement of a truth more profound. Does anything have existence *if it is not experienced through another?* Is there a sound without an ear to interpret it, or a tree without an eye to see it or a hand to feel it?

Is there a me, if I am not experiencing something beyond myself, or if I am not being experienced by another? I can only talk about who I am in terms of how I relate to my physical world and the people whom I touch.

I've always known who I am. I'm the daughter who worked in her father's store and helped her mother raise younger brothers and sisters. I'm the student who got good grades in school. I'm the mother who gave birth to six children and has loved and cherished each since the moment of their conception. I'm the breadwinner, cook, chauffeur, comforter. I'm the writer trying to touch others. I'm the sometimes-loner, who loves to walk in the sand on the beach. I'm the etc.-woman, who sews her wardrobe, who enjoys conversations with friends, who can get emotional over great music and cry at an opera, etc., etc. I'm the child of my Father in heaven.

Some people would argue with me, saying I am describing "roles", not "identity." Nonsense. Motherhood, wifehood, job-holding, chore-doing are not role playing but the reality of living. When I cook and wash, transport my children and dialogue about their problems, I am not playing a mother-role. I am *being a mother*—a living, breathing, loving person.

Perhaps the sudden, rampant epidemic of identity-crisis among people is simply a case of confusion. Each of us has a need to be unique, to be loved, to be understood, to be left alone at times, to be served at times, to grow according to our talents. When these needs are not being met, we may feel exploited and cry out, "What about me?"

But in the very question, we are proclaiming our value, and thus affirming our identity. The crisis, as I see it, is not our identity, but our *situation.*

When our situation improves, it's amazing how fast we can "find ourselves."

And our situation improves once we tailor-make answers to five crucial questions and begin acting on these, with determination:

What do you want for yourself?

What do you hope to achieve today—and tomorrow?

Are these reasonable and fair desires and goals?

What obstacles stand in your way of achieving these?

What are you going to do about removing the obstacles?

First step is to begin taking responsibility for ourselves. No one else can do this for us. Next, the new life requires self-reeducation, focusing on what we have and not on our deprivations, and accepting the reality of our current place.

You will experience, at times, boredom, and internal agitation; bleak moments and scary ones; failures and successes, too. Most of all, there will be change in you.

I know because I've been there. I have felt the self-respect and confidence and exhilarating knowledge that even if the days are on the dark side today, I can work at making them turn around tomorrow. Dull? Bright? It doesn't matter. The days are ours. We are the important ones now—the movers charting the directions of our lives ourselves.

Chapter 9
You and Sex

In the early 1970's, Sister Thelma Hall, a Roman Catholic Cenacle nun, and I started the first organization for Divorced and Separated Catholics ever to exist in my diocese. It was also one of the first such groups to be formed anywhere in the country.

From the beginning, Sister Thelma and I agreed that the Program of Concern, as she named it, would be open to both men and women. We knew this might be criticized, given the Catholic Church's firm position of not allowing remarriage for Catholics who have terminated their "valid" marriages. At that time, I was working as a reporter for *The Long Island Catholic,* the official weekly newspaper of the Rockville Centre Diocese. My job kept me in contact with many of the priests who worked in the Chancery office as administrators of one program or another. A few months after Divorced and Separated Catholics began meeting, one of the priests (a man much younger than myself) who was involved with diocesan religious education, stopped me and said:

"I have some reservations about that being a mixed group. There's always the possibility of dating and that would cause those Catholics to be tempted to fornication."

I looked at him in absolute disbelief. "Father," I countered, "of course there's the possibility that a divorced man coming to the Cenacle meetings might be attracted to a divorced woman, and they might decide to have a date. But did it ever occur to you that if people want to date, if they really feel the need for heterosexual companionship, they *will* date, with or without the Cenacle program—or the consent of the Church?"

I couldn't believe that he actually thought keeping Catholic men and women separated in church groups would keep them celibate. His position was as naive as the old Snow White song, "Wishing Will Make It So." To add to my annoyance, his very use of the word "fornication" had repulsed me. The only expression that turns me off more is referring to the relationship between remarried Catholics as "adulterous." Whether it fits into prescribed dogmas of the Church, cultural patterns or social mores, the plain fact is that few grown adult men and women, living in the real world, are going to be able to suppress their normal sexual needs. What's more important, few are going to want to.

For the single parent, once sexually active, or at least sexually experienced, the absence of this form of communication presents a new and especially difficult problem in his or her new, non-partnered status. It needs to be faced honestly and then analyzed discreetly, acted on discreetly and carried out discreetly because, like it or not, sex in single parenting becomes a family hurdle.

Think for a moment about the new situation from the perspective of the children who are newly living with just a mother. If they are very young, they'll give indications now and then that they miss not having a man around the house. "When is daddy coming home?" is a question single mothers of very young children are often asked. Very soon, they get precocious enough to ask, "Are you going to find another daddy for me?" They're indicating loud and clear that they have Daddy on their mind. The first man they see with Mommy becomes, potentially, "daddy.' Conversely, the first woman dated by single fathers becomes "mommy."

If young children see this new "daddy" or "mommy"

sleeping in their parent's bed, the parent-conclusion becomes even more solidified. If the relationship turns out to be
transient, and a new stranger comes in, starting the cycle
over again, young children not only become confused; their
trust is shattered as they readjust again and again to a
deserting "parent."

Single parents may feel they have a right to sexual
attachments but they should make these choices with their
eyes open to the fact that what they do has strong repercussions within their family. Single parenthood is not an au-
tonomous state. It is a you-me relationship which needs
gentle nurturing even as, individually, parents may try to find
lost and needed intimacy with another, and probably, temporary, partner.

When children are older, they're wondering about
Mom—or Dad—on a different level. They may not connect
any of her needs with sex—simply because it's hard for most
kids to visualize their parents in bed for any other reason than
sleeping—but they certainly begin to wonder about what
Mom does for fun, particularly if Mom stays home during all
her non-working hours.

While your own children may not be thinking about your
sex life, you might be surprised at how often their friends are.
"Does your mother date?" is a common question asked by
girl friends. I remember nearly falling off my chair once when
my daughter related a conversation with a friend who had
asked this question about my dating.

"I don't think so," Margaret replied. "She's never brought a
guy to the house."

"If she doesn't date, that's not normal."

"Well, I *think* my mother's normal."

"I bet she's not. I bet she doesn't date because she's a
lesbian."

After I stopped laughing, I thought about the incident. What
the girl was implying, in spite of her wrong conclusion, had a
certain basic truth. She was really saying that sex is such an
important facet of a person's existence, that no one can
ignore it.

As a single parent, you have to face the question of what
sex means to you personally and find an answer that works

for you in your present situation. From talking to many new singles over the years, I have discovered that the greatest deprivation is not sexual pleasure, but companionship and intimacy. Their sexual needs are tied up with their need to alleviate loneliness. Dr. Joyce Brothers, the noted psychologist and columnist, once reported a survey disclosing that most married women sought sexual relations with their husbands as a way to be "cuddled." The beauty of the sexual act was its intimacy and after glow of well-being stemming from the comfort of being lovingly touched by another person. This is the void in so many single parent's lives.

What do you do as a single person with sexual needs, who also happens to be a solitary parent? Do you work at preserving a personal sense of privacy for this component of your life, keeping it sheltered from the probing eyes and questions of the children? Or do you level with them about where you stand on this subject, and, if you choose to date, do it openly?

I can't answer that for anyone else but myself. I can talk, however, about some of the sexual hurdles you face as a single person/parent.

Society's new liberal moral standards, particularly if these are in conflict with your personal standards, can be a major pain. Recently I was talking to a young man, newly divorced because his wife had opted for the single life again. He's trying to overcome his loneliness, but finds the dating scene unappealing.

"Every time you date a girl these days, she expects the evening to end in bed," he told me. "If I tell them I'm not interested in having sex with a virtual stranger, that I'd rather have some conversation and companionship, they look at me as if I'm completely abnormal, or at least insane!"

I used to think only women had that problem. Not true. Today, any person who has moral standards which exclude free and casual sex finds him or herself regarded as something akin to a circus freak. Many singles who do live by personal values or religious beliefs that forbid sexual intimacy outside of marriage, find that they cannot date at all if they want to adhere to their beliefs.

"It's too much of a hurdle to spend an evening defending my right not to go to bed with a guy just because he happened to buy me a dinner," said one woman, adding, "I've simply stopped dating men. I go out now occasionally with women from the office where I work."

Another new experience for the single parent is the discovery that you are now a subject of great curiosity. "Does she or doesn't she?" people ask, and they're not talking about whether you dye your hair. Suddenly, everybody assumes they have the right to become a Peeping Tom where you are concerned. They ask—Are you dating? Do you go to singles bars? Do you believe in swinging? Would you go to a man's apartment? Do you sleep around with anybody—or are you fussy? Do you sleep with just one guy—and is he married?

"None of your business" has become a standard line in my vocabulary. That doesn't stop the questions. It merely changes them to—

"You're still young and attractive. You should have a husband. Why don't you find a man and marry again?"

That one I sometimes answer. I say, maybe. Maybe sometime way in the future, when my children are all grown and I'm feeling *aloneness,* I might think about how my life would change—for better and worse—with marriage.

That answer doesn't satisfy anyone, because what people are really asking is, Don't you miss sex if you're not having any? Are you having sex and keeping it a big secret?

All of this has led me to conclude that the logo of our sex-drenched society is certainly anatomical—a gigantic nose.

The newly single woman also is in a target position for men who like to engage in the game of conquest, where both players end up in bed. The old fashioned word for this very old game is "propositioning." It is played and dealt with in a variety of ways. Many single mothers tell me this is a frequent problem they meet, with the majority of men being married coworkers, or occasionally, even neighbors or relatives.

I must point out that what makes a proposition particularly repelling is that it is an invitation to a particular kind of one-night-stand, skin-sex. It is rarely the offer to begin a fine, long-lasting, loving relationship. In my 11 years of single-hood, I have been propositioned only rarely. I'm not sure if I'm bragging or complaining, but I think my low incidence of encounters with would-be accommodating males verifies my belief that each of us sends out unconscious signals about our behavior standards. My signals apparently indicate that I don't mess around, so don't waste your time.

Just for fun, these are a few variations of the proposition game that I've had to deal with:

Traditional Proposition is blah, unimaginative and as tired as an old cliché. The lines are familiar. Haven't we met somewhere before? Weren't you a waitress once at Lorenzo's? What kind of perfume are you wearing—it's driving me crazy. I know a place you'd love where they serve . . . (anything) . . .

I was taking a course a few years ago in Perspectives In Molecular Biology and a young man was assigned to be my lab partner. Before long, he invited me to have a cup of coffee with him after class. That sounded harmless enough. But before the brew was cold, I was getting the old line about how he'd like to talk to me over dinner the next night because I seemed so warm and intelligent and he was having trouble with his wife who didn't understand him.

Knowing I was getting the old traditional proposition, I took out a pencil and paper and wrote down three names.

"These are marriage counsellors," I said. "If you are having problems with your wife, they can help. I can't. If, however, you're really looking for comfort instead of help, you'll have to find another shoulder."

He never came back to class. I hope it was because he was busy patching things up with his wife and not just suffering from damaged ego.

The Intellectual Proposition is devious. Here the seeker attempts to get your attention by starting a discussion. It can be anything from Aristotle to Watergate at first. Everything is punctuated with how intelligent you are and how refreshing it is to find a woman who enjoys a head-contact. A lunch or dinner date is proposed to continue the discussion. Eventually, you get to Catullus on Love, to Erich Fromm on The Art of Loving, and then an analysis of the latest sex-movie from

Sweden. When you get to the subject of how beautiful a free act of love is between two mature people, it's getting very late. You are being seduced.

The Proposition By Flattery is mean. Everybody likes to be told they're attractive, nice, doing a fine job at their profession, admirable, courageous, clever and so on. At a subtle point, however, the flattery may turn out to have a catch.

I was being interviewed once by a magazine editor who wanted to learn more about my observations of Marriage Encounter, since I had written a book on the subject. He played around a lot with a tape recorder, flattered me considerably, but never actually got around to doing a decent interview. Finally, he said, with just a touch of boyish innocence,

"You have me kind of shook. I didn't expect anything like this. It happens now and then with me—that I meet a woman and know the chemistry is right."

Naturally, he wanted to reschedule the interview over cocktails. I told him the end product of many chemical connections is a lot of hot air. I was never again available to him for an interview.

The Shy Guy Proposition is designed to arouse your curiosity and make you nervous at the same time. He's someone you run into a bit too often. He says nothing, smiles and stares. I met one of these types (who are almost always married) in, of all places, a religious discussion group. After several weeks of being stared at, naturally I broke down and started a conversation.

"Why are you always staring at me?" I asked.

"Your face is so alive," he said, trying to sound like Omar Shariff, I think. "I'm so glad you spoke first. I didn't have the nerve—"

I did an absolutely unforgiveable thing. I laughed. "Well yes, my face is alive because it is connected to my head bone, connected to my neck bone, connected to my shoulder bone, connected to—"

The trouble with shy guys is they have no sense of humor.

The Brash Proposition is the one I detest. This guy gets right to the bottom line. When you say no, he sneeringly counters with, "What are you saving it for, baby?"

I have answered, equally bluntly, "Not for you, buster."

The real problem, of course, is not how to handle a proposition. That's simple. It's yes or no, and it's your decision. The real challenge is learning how to live as a single person with normal sexual needs and desires while at the same time sharing this life of ours, from housing to loving, with children.

The decisions we make cannot result from external or societal pressures to behave in a certain way. We must make them out of our own accepted value system, our own consciences. If we make decisions to act in a manner contrary to our moral beliefs, we attempt to live a contradiction. That is self-destructive.

In all honesty, I must underscore that sexual expression or repression is a personal choice. I would never presume to tell another person how to live, nor would I ever condemn a person for his or her behavioral choices, except where this behavior explicitly hurts or exploits another. I have had many discussions with single parents about the sexual problems we face. Many have vastly different values from my own, and in no way would I attempt to sell them mine. As an example, one woman strongly disputed my rebuff of propositioning males. She even said I was cold and cruel. Her position was, and I quote, "Sometimes you just need a good screw and you don't care who gives it to you."

I respect her right to believe that but personally I would buy the Brooklyn bridge before that one.

For myself, and this is my own, very personal position which I am not suggesting is "right" for anyone else but me—sex has meaning only in terms of embellishing human importance and dignity. I have always believed that physical sex is a beautiful union only in the context of enduring love between two people. I have stood by this belief and have been called brainwashed, old-fashioned, not with it, and just plain nuts. No matter. I know I am an idealist about sex. I also know I choose to remain one.

I've had young women tell me, "I wouldn't have sex with a guy unless I knew he cared about me." What does that mean, really? He probably cares about cats and dogs and pizzas, too. They've said, "My friends would think I'm some kind of kook if I treated myself like a virgin." But is that a good reason for physical intimacy? Isn't that really the worst kind of coercion? What about your right to make decisions for yourself?

I've heard women say, "I'm sexually free because I'm liberated," and then they let a man move in with them and proceed to cook his meals, wash his clothes and pay half or more of the bills for the privilege. I'd say, isn't this a phony freedom for a woman? Isn't the only thing free in this setup the free ride given to the man? What price is being paid by the children who are getting daily messages from this kind of arrangement, which I would wager, are not positive at all?

I've come to the conclusion that basically there are two kinds of sex. One is a bad scene and the other is a magnificent scenario. One exploits and is an ending from the time it starts; the other nourishes and continually generates beginnings.

The first kind, sex without the promise of love-forever, is the worst kind of poverty, for it pretends to offer closeness while strengthening aloneness. It leaves people vulnerable to shattering psychological repercussions when rejection takes place. A college professor once told me that he had become completely opposed to premarital living together because no two people were ready to call off an affair at the same time. After dealing with countless rejected and discarded "partners", and trying to help them sew the splinters of themselves back together and regain a decent self-image, he had become strongly opposed to these popular sex liasons.

The second kind of sex provides the milieu for people who not only have a vision of themselves as important, valuable, and redeemed, but also have experienced the fantastic beauty of knowing that someone else shares this vision—a one-to-one connection with all the sparks soaring out.

I think too often we've narrowed sex down to the conflict of pleasure vs. procreation and argued its morality from these two corners. That still separates sex from love and human dignity. I do not see virtue either in sexual pleasure or pregnancy if either condition results from a physical act not dignified by love.

When two people love each other enough to want it to be

permanent, enough to vow to lay their lives on the line for each other, offering utter fidelity—a love to the death—then sex between them can become what every person is looking for: the ultimate vehicle for transcending the isolation of self, where the union is complete because every act holds out the promise that there is more of love to come, another star to land on. Then you are whole—together—and sex has meaning.

Sex without commitment, like service stations, will no doubt continue to flourish, with people ever searching for whatever it is they need and think such sex will bring them. That is, I repeat, their judgment and choice and I do not criticize them. But my value system will not let me separate sex from the covenant of love and fidelity. It is the only vision of sex which makes sense to me personally.

I would guess that I am not alone in holding to my values when it comes to a behavioral expression of sex. Proof exists in the frequency with which the following question comes up at single parents meetings: "Where can you find unattached good men and women?"

Sometimes we run the risk of getting cynical, answering, "Mostly in your dreams." The greater risk is the counter-question, "Is the single life really a deficient life? Do we have to have an intimate attachment to another person?"

A new book called *How To Get A Man After You're Forty* (Crown Publishers) advises you not to hold your breath waiting for Mr. Right if you're at that age. What bothers me about the book—which is actually an excellent and humorous treatise on how to get to like yourself—is its title. It is one more addition to the prevalent belief that if a woman doesn't have a man she has no flesh on her ribs.

Somewhere between this position and the ultra feminist one which proclaims "A woman without a man is like a fish without a bicycle" is a middle ground. It is a balance point between these two ends of desperation where life revolves around must-have and wouldn't-have a man/woman. You are in balance when you learn how to juggle your physical, emotional and spiritual needs without letting any one of them dominate. In this position, you can be in charge of your behavior while you figure out rationally what direction you are choosing as the best one for you, given your history, responsibilities, values and goals.

Sexual behavior is one of the first and maybe the most compelling choices you'll have to make. Our options are the same as those faced by any other singles.

Celibacy is one choice. We can say, simply, no sex without a demonstrated commitment of fidelity on the part of a lover. Admittedly, this is tough, but not impossible. In a somewhat obvious way, the very lifestyle of a single parent can act as a cold shower. It's hard to think romantic thoughts when you're exhausted from working on the job or at home dealing with childrens' problems. Celibacy works best if your motivation is strong. People with firm religious values, upward mobility in work goals, or who are dedicated to helping people in other-centered professions stand a better chance of success in living as celibates.

Some singles choose to become "mistresses" to a particular man, or "lovers" of a particular woman. This is a tension-laden dead end, and always holds the possibility of personal damage to one's self-image and sense of self-worth. It also is a relationship of injustice to the legitimate spouse, and this makes this kind of liason highly suspect morally. Why would anyone make this sexual behavior choice? Reasons I have been given include—

"It just happens." "He's a wonderful guy" (even though he's cheating on his wife). "It's very safe—she can't make any demands on me." "It's the best of both worlds, like courtship. I have an attentive lover who cares about me. I'm not bed hopping."

Occasionally they tell you the negative side, the sudden cancellation of planned trysts because "something came up at home;" the secrecy and hiding so that his wife or her husband, and friends and co-workers won't find out.

Another choice, already mentioned several times, is bar-hopping, swinging, taking casual lovers and engaging in various forms of stop-and-shop sex. This probably works for a great many people, easing their sexual tensions and giving them no conscience conflicts or self-worth problems.

Shortly after I began writing this book, I had lunch with a divorced Catholic man in his 40's. He is a church-going

Catholic and a lector in his parish. In a very open manner, he showed me a photo of his "latest" girl friend. I asked him how he reconciled his sexual behavior with his religion, since the Catholic Church forbids sexual activity outside of marriage. He had no conflict at all, he said. To deny this expression of his humanity would be destructive to him and would therefore be a greater evil than not living strictly by the letter of church law. I would not presume to challenge him on this, since he obviously was acting without conscience conflict.

I have been told that some single parents turn to lesbianism or homosexuality. I know of only one such situation. In private conversations, some others admit to finding sexual relief through occasional masturbation.

Finally, remarriage remains as the most accepted choice in restoring a balanced normal sexual life. This is an answer for many but not for all of us.

This chapter is certainly not a treatise on sex, nor in any way an attempt to compete with the million or so books and manuals which must exist on the subject. It is simply my personal discussion of an important problem to be faced when a person who once opted for a marriage-union with all its meanings, finds that dream now gone—while the desires that produced it remain as strong as ever.

As persons, we have the right to find new ways of easing our loneliness and our physical urgings for closeness with a mate. As parents, our choices will be reflected in our homes and children.

We have to pay attention to this fact.

Chapter 10
Dealing with Your Energy Crisis

It was early March and still very cold. I had come into work as usual at 8 a.m. though I felt listless that morning. By 10 a.m., I was exhausted. Within an hour, I was sure that I was coming down with something, and giving in for a change, I took the rest of the day off, charging it to sick time.

When I got home it was too much of a chore even to make a cup of coffee. I collapsed on the couch, feeling oddly bitter and uninspired. The phone rang, jarring me, and I kind of drifted down the stairs to answer it.

"Toni?" asked the cheerful voice. "Am I in luck to find you home!"

It was an old friend of mine, an editor for a house organ magazine, with offices in New York City.

"I'm in a bind," she said. "I need an article for this next issue, with a one-week deadline. You're the only one I know that I can depend on to do a good job on this and meet such a tight deadline. Could you fit this into your schedule?"

After a 15-minute conversation, I had not only agreed to do the piece, I had also decided to get on the next train to the city and make the necessary phone calls and research that very afternoon.

I was sitting on the train before I had the chance to think about my sudden transformation from the drooped and wilted "getting a virus" woman I had been an hour before, to the sophisticated, energy-laden professional I now felt myself to be. I could visualize myself in before-and-after photos on the back page of a magazine advertising some potent capsule that perfomed energy-producing miracles in humans. It struck me as very funny.

The incident also taught me a great deal about the meaning of energy and fatigue. Obviously, I wasn't getting a virus. My exhaustion was due to other causes—curable ones, instantly curable in fact, given a prescription which works on the real cause of the fatigue.

On the train I had time to analyze the events leading to the day's incident. For weeks I had been trapped in a mundane, non-writing assignment on my regular job. The day before, I had been stuck, literally, as a "servant" to a demanding, impolite wife of a visiting guest of the university where I am employed. I found this particularly distasteful because the way I viewed her, she got her status only from being Mrs. Doctor so and so, not because of any of her own personal achievements. What right did she have to treat me in a demeaning manner? I actually felt superior to her, because anything I owned in life, including my title, I had earned, along with providing a gocd life for my children. I resented everything as that day wore on—my job, my bosses, my children, my life . . .

Any amateur psychologist could quickly analyze that my build-up of boredom and resentment had caused my exhaustion. When my friend called, complimenting me as a writer, my self respect was instantly sitmulated, shaking out the underlying anger and stimulating my dormat energy potential.

This kind of before-and-after change happens often enough in our lives to make "energy" a most interesting subject of analysis. Usually the change is not as dramatic as the one I just related. Mostly, we call it getting a "second wind." That's a common phenomenon which serves to keep us in balance between the unpleasant, energy-draining tasks in life and the pleasant, energy-restoring ones. When, however, the exhausted "before" is never followed by a perked up "after", that's trouble.

Energy is such a common word, used every day to describe the way in which our world is powered. When the source of power breaks down, we have an energy-crisis. Everybody understands this.

More difficult to understand is that human energy—our personal power source—breaks down, too. When we experience a personal energy-crisis the results are terribly parallel to an environmental one. We are shut down, immobilized, with blackness all around us.

Single parents are unusually susceptible to experiencing periodic, or even frequent, personal power failures with resulting bleakness. The crisis is manifested mainly by fatigue, which is different from plain tiredness. Fatigue is tiredness gone travelling, like an amoeba, to sap away at every bit of energy in your body.

Fatigue comes in threes. First is *nice fatigue*—which follows something you really enjoyed, even if you overdid it—like spending a day in the city, shopping in the afternoon, attending an evening Broadway musical and driving back home at midnight.

Then there's *plain fatigue*—which follows an ordinary day's work, with too many extra jobs thrown in.

The third is *no-kidding fatigue,* the once-in-a-while depth-core stuff, accompanied by an isolated, uncared-for feeling, maybe headache and dizziness, anxiety and an unwillingness to move.

No-kidding fatigue is the tough one because to relieve this, you have to identify what's bothering you. It may be a simple pileup of work, summed in the familiar phrase, "I can't get out from under", or it might have its roots in boredom, emotions, resentments and other psychological factors.

As I have indicated several times earlier in this book, the very responsibilities of the lifestyle of single parenthood are inordinately taxing on the one person who has to keep all the pieces in place. Sometimes the pressure buildup on a single parent is too subtle to recognize until an emergency erupts. Sometimes it is being suppressed with the parent's attitude being, "if I ignore it, it will go away."

One divorced mother of three young children, after six months of struggle during which she had to move from her lovely one-family home into a cheap apartment, find a job and try to care for her children, gave an admirable appearance of being able to handle her extraordinary change in lifestyle—until she ended up in the hospital with a bleeding ulcer. I knew another mother who kept ignoring her fatigue until one of her children fell off a bike and had to be hospitalized. She collapsed at that point, drained of all energy, and was temporarily unable to cope with her life.

What is energy? When is it used well? What drains it?

The old textbook definition said that energy is the ability to do work. That's probably still the best all-round definition. The answer to whether it is underutilized, overutilized or just plain drained out is harboured in the word "ability." Normally, we should be able to draw out from ourselves the power needed both to get our multi-jobs done and to do other kinds of activities, labelled recreation, fun, exercise, escapism, and so forth. That's a balance which, in effect, recharges the batteries of our energy sources. When we are not able to keep this balance, we stand in danger of losing our very ability to "work" at all. The old wise saying was that "all work and no play makes Jack a dull boy." That can be paraphrased to apply to the single parent:

"Overwork, with no rest and recreation, makes a parent a dulled person."

Symptoms of a personal energy crisis may vary from parent to parent, but common ones exist.

You feel overwhelmed, a sense of being smothered or drowning. The odds against you are too much. You can't get out from under. Everywhere you look, the signs are there to remind you of the trap. You are engulfed in unfinished work on your job, in the house and with your children; letters not written; bills not paid; wash piling up; children not getting enough attention; personal appearance ignored. You begin to become conscious of language and communication problems. You may stutter a little, repeat yourself, forget that you've already said what you're about to say again.

At this stage, you probably begin to experience excesssive

fatigue, digestive upsets, or even continuous "cold" symptoms. Your ability to make decisions is weakening. You don't want to do anything but sleep or watch television. The occasional self-suggestion that you should get dressed up and out to a lecture or movie is battered down with an immediate counterattack of "that's too much trouble."

This fatigue brings a new worry that your body and mind are being taken over by a creeping, spreading malaise that's going to end up ruining you. Your work will not get done; you won't get paid; the family which is so dependent on you will suffer. You now begin to wish your life away—dreaming that if it were only five years from now, the children would be older, some, maybe, even on their own; life would be easier— better—and you could breathe again.

This is a personal energy crisis, and it is real, brought on by trying to do what is humanly impossible—trying to put two quarts of substance into a one quart container. You have been driven, not by common sense, but by a determination to "make it". alone, characterized by "I can, and if I can't, I *will*."

The causes of a personal energy crisis in a single parent are multiple.

Plain overwork is the major culprit. You can't expect to keep up a pace that is humanly destructive. If you're in the position I've been talking about in this book—chief cook, bottlewasher, breadwinner, in short, chief EVERYTHING— you run the risk of trying to squeeze 30 hours into 20. It can't be done. I know. I've tried it. I spent nearly two years working my regular job, working every evening trying to keep the house waxed and polished, constantly providing rides for the children—the suburban mother's nightmare—attending their school functions, and picking up the pencil at about 11 p.m. to put in two or three more hours in my moonlighting job of producing articles for a syndicate at $30 per. I began to visualize myself like a character from a Max Sennet comedy, running around in an accelerated condition from the time I got up in the morning until I dissolved about 2 a.m.

One day a friend asked me, "How do you manage to get everything done?"

"Because I never stop," I answered, without even hesitating to think about her question.

Once I had verbalized that idiocy, I resolved to begin unwinding. It was a long, slow, not always successful project, but I did, at least, avert a nervous breakdown, ulcers, high blood pressure and some of the other goodies that result from pressured overwork.

An energy breakdown can be caused by physical self-neglect, not eating properly, not getting enough sleep, lack of recreation. Mothers are notorious junk eaters. Working mothers are, in addition, meal rushers and meal skippers. Single parents are also in danger of developing bad eating habits during times they are undergoing emotional stresses. Fatigue is often just the body kicking up a fuss because it is nutritionally poor.

The attempt to do "everything" for your children is a single-parent trap. It is usually a reaction to guilt. We feel guilty because our children have no live-in father or mother, and so we attempt to overcompensate for that void by trying to fill it ourselves. This can demand more energy than we have to give. For example, one mother with three sons who liked sports, knocked herself out playing baseball with one, softball with another and tennis with the third. When she sprained her wrist, it was the proverbial blessing in disguise. It gave her two week's "vacation" from her near terminal fatigue and time for her to examine whether it was really her job to be a physical "father" to her sons.

Worry is another energy drainer. Someone said once that "worry is the interest you pay on money you never had." You can ruin your today worrying about tomorrow—but what a waste and how exhausting!

Noise can wear you down, too. When you're a working single parent, you come home just as tired as the husband next door—but with a difference. He comes home to a clean house, a set table, a meal cooked and ready to be served to him. You come home to clean, set the table, do the cooking and the serving. That's when you discover that little feet go clod-clod, not pitter-patter. You get weary from the sounds of walking, talking, TV, rock music, piano practice, telephone ringing, the creaking of the refrigerator as it is constantly raided, and slamming doors. You don't need a psychiatrist to tell you that noise saps your energy and that the sounds of silence are refreshing.

Some single parents can be too "other centered." Taking on too much responsibility for the children is a mistake. I found this an easy trap for myself, as I mentioned in an earlier chapter. I felt that rather than add pressure to the lives of my children, I should be the one to take on extra chores and make *their* lives easier, not harder. It would add to my exhaustion but it wouldn't kill me to come home from work, cook, do the dishes, the wash, the cleaning, give them money for concerts, etc., all "justified" because they had homework to do, needed a social life, or would be terribly inconvenienced by the chore in question.

When I learned to get out from under my guilt cloak and temper my attraction for martyrdom, I saw quite clearly that when a family is in a tough situation together, everybody has to be occasionally uncomfortable together—or you stop being a real family. A mother-saviour is characterized by exhaustion, which makes her a drag. Children may try to get out of doing dishes, babysitting, working a part-time job, but if you say "no, fair is fair, and we all pull a weight together" in the long run your firmness works in your favor. Children learn self-respect and respect for you—a parent who refuses to be exploited by children, who has some energy left to be a fun mother instead of a drained out blob.

Spending too much time worrying about the elusive "tomorrow" is another exhaustion device. One young mother I knew wasted her evenings with a paper and pencil, plotting and planning her hours and budget for weeks in advance. She never really reached the order and efficiency she craved. She merely became continually exhausted and confused due to frustration over unexpected complications and unrealistic projections. I reminded her one day that in the bible, the Lord gave us good advice about not overdoing the tomorrow bit. "Sufficient for the day is its own trials," said Jesus. This was sound advice then and ever since.

Unresolved angers and resentments take a tremendous toll on the body, robbing it of needed energy and blocking the ability to draw on reserve energy supplies. The personal example I related at the beginning of this chapter points this out. One mother said she began to suspect an emotional problem when she found herself becoming utterly fatigued every Saturday, beginning around late morning. Saturday was the one day out of the week her ex-husband was supposed to take the two children out for the day. Very often, however, he would call about noontime and give some excuse as to why he couldn't make it that day. Her plans for shopping or going to the hair dresser or simply having some time to herself would be immediately changed by his call. She one day explained,

"I realized that my fatigue developed out of resentment and anger anticipating that he might call and mess up my Saturday. I needed some free hours once a week and I was furious when he stole them from me by retreating from his responsibility. Since I didn't want the children to see me angry, I thought I was controlling myself well. Instead, my body coped with the resentment and anger in a different way—exhaustion."

Monotony and boredom can cause tremendous fatigue. Single parents have a heavier workload than most people and it might be hard for someone not in that situation to understand how the life can be monotonous when it is so busy. Easy. It's not hard work or even an abundance of work that fells a person. It is sameness, with unsufficient "breaks" taken as needed battery-recharging time. If you find yourself overcome with a malaise that blocks you from carrying out a plan of work, particularly on weekends, you could well suspect the cause to be boredom. You have to force yourself at times deliberately to make a decision *not* to clean house on Saturday, but to go out and have your hair done instead; or take the children on a picnic; or cancel Susie's piano lesson. Boredom is sneaky and can overtake everybody's life without warning. Like any other illness, it is personal, confined within your person, making you the only one who can fight it.

Poverty is exhausting, too. Poverty keeps you trapped in your boredom because having no money is a very effective obstacle to getting your hair done, or going on a picnic or providing piano lessons for your child. Poverty is learning 50 ways to make rice and hamburger; living with a faded and dated wardrobe; saying "sorry" all too often to the children's requests; protecting your privacy so people won't know how bad things really are with you financially; watching the house fall apart as needed repairs stay undone; seeing yourself in a black hole, with hope jaded.

I have known many, many single mothers trying to raise families on a few hundred dollars a month. Many of them become listless, manifesting many symptoms of illness. The culprit is not a virus, but poverty.

Conflict is a very serious energy stealer. I can pinpoint the times when I felt I would never get out of bed again. In almost every case, these were times when I was undergoing a conflict situation either on my job or with one of my children. I remember when my second son, John, wanted to buy a motorcycle as a teenager. I was terrified at the thought, being convinced that a disproportionate number of fatal road accidents involve cyclists. He almost wore me down with his arguments, but I would not relent. When he was 18, he saved enough money to buy one. When he brought the thing home, I was furious, felt he had defied me, believed that he was taking advantage of not having an authoritarian father around to clobber him for disobedience. The conflict exhausted me. I knew that since he was 18, it was unreasonable to fight him or try to stop him from using it. Besides, I was so tired from years of arguing anti-motorcycle that I couldn't handle any more of it. Yet, I had to resolve the conflict—a situation erupting often enough in families when what a parent sees as proper behavior for children is challenged by them.

There's an old saying, "If you can't fight 'em, join 'em." I had John take me for a ride on the motorcycle, an experience which convinced me that if he drove carefully, he possibly would be as safe, or unsafe, as I am in my car. When I got rid of the conflict, my exhaustion left.

Finally, I have known some very tired single parents who got that way for no particular reason at all. They mope around simply because they are locked in a pervading sense of unhappiness about their current lot in life. If you suggest to them that they get out of the house and do something to spark their life, they give varying responses like, why? who cares? what difference does it make? I'm not interested, and other sarcasms. Their discontent may be understandable, but it can't be justified. It is within everyone's power to change their lives—if only a tiny bit. No one has to stay locked in unhappiness. It is at least worth the effort to try to restore yourself to life.

Recognizing the many causes of your personal energy depletion comes first, but this recognition must be followed by a willingness to do something about the condition so as to rid yourself of the fatigue-disease. Since most energy-failure is due to overwork, the starting point for most single parents is to admit that you have to slow down, or suffer the consequences.

Dr. Joyce Brothers has often made the point that "relaxation is a necessity, not a luxury." She says too many people suffer from "hurry sickness", throwing themselves into high tension and stress conditions. People have to clear their minds and relax their bodies, or they are well into psychosomatic illness—physical disease stemming from emotional causes.

Single parents, prone to "hurry sickness", have to reprogram their days, eliminating some of the activities of the old life to make way for the demands of the new.

I learned to lower my housekeeping standards. As one example, curtains and windows get done before Christmas and during early summer, and not each season as I used to. I also de-cluttered my house. I can get more tired from looking at a mess than from doing something about it, so I decided that house *clearing* came before house *cleaning* and I threw out every nonessential. I stopped starting projects which now, it seemed, I could never finish. I found it depressing to keep bumping into half-sewn dresses, a half painted room and an ironing board which was always standing. I refused to get trapped into long phone conversations which, for me, were energy sappers. I learned how to make faster decisions about choosing chores to be done. Whenever I felt bewildered, asking myself, "what shall I do first—the wash, the shopping, the writing, the sewing?", I changed the question to, "What absolutely has to get done this morning?"

Each single parent has to work at how to use time more efficiently and effectively. I've learned that you can cut out, cut down and cut down more. For example, I have gradually cut down ironing to the point where the board comes out about once a month, thanks to being very careful about reading washing instruction labels on all the clothes and linens I buy. Baking is now a rare chore, except for holidays and special events. I've learned to cook one pot of rice and use it as the basis for different suppers on three consecutive nights, saving a lot of cooking time.

I write letters and read books and magazines during the odd minutes of the day—early morning, at lunch, right after dinner, in waiting rooms, on the train. If I wait to have a "block of time" for these tasks, they'd never get done.

A most effective preventive of exhaustion is learning to utilize the strength of a very tiny word—*no*. That was the hardest segment of my reprogramming but I've learned how to say it. In the past month I've said no to a number of invitations to serve a good cause: a local branch of the American Cancer Society wanted me to work on their public relations committee; a friend asked me to join a Women's Political Caucus; and I politely declined giving a talk on Catholic Single Parents in a nearby parish.

There was a time when probably I would have said yes to all of these. I had properly conditioned myself to "serve" so much that I treated almost every overtly altruistic movement, cause or group as an offer I couldn't refuse, even when I didn't have all the data. Now I think differently. Time isn't a commodity, something you pass around like cake. Time is the substance of life. When anyone asks you to give your time, they're asking for a chunk of your life. Once I realized that, I started getting fussy about what I would give chunks of my life to, even at the risk of appearing snooty and feeling guilty.

Admittedly, few of us can live our days exactly as we would choose. For me, choices have boiled down to value. If I see no value, or little value, in what I'm doing or have been asked to do, I stop. Many a day I would prefer not to go to work, or face an unpleasant writing job. But my job has value. It feeds, clothes and gives shelter to me and my children. Sometimes I hate to drive the kids to music lessons, stores, sports events, etc. But I value their development and so such things are worth my time—a chunk of my life.

Where I have learned to draw the line is when *other people* decide how I should spend my time—uninvited guests, meetings to promote causes in which I have no interest, social invitations which I could care less about.

The combination of reducing the activities filling my life, plus the self-satisfaction of being assertive enough to make my own choices about how I am going to spend my time, has been a great energy restorer.

Another step a single parent might be able to take to reduce fatigue is to get some help, if at all possible. The Lord said, "Ask and you shall receive," but we don't believe it because our experience with the real world is the opposite. Yet, I've found that very often, the single parent in need of help has never actually asked a neighbor or relative for a temporary assist. Too often, pride or a fear of refusal prevents us from even trying to get help. I'm not talking about developing a dependency on others. That would be wrong for all parties, givers and takers. But occasionally, getting some help like free babysitting, transportation, handyman aid or housekeeping services could act like a tonic. In my case, an essential need for me has been to have two weeks each summer alone, with the responsibility of the children completely lifted from my back. My sister, Jeanette, herself a single mother with three young children, has taken my children into her home each summer to give me that opportunity to take my much needed break. Her help, and even more, the empathy and love which motivates it, renews me, refreshes me and restores my energy.

If you find your exhaustion confined to certain hours of the day, the cause may be quite normal, simply evidence of your physical peaks and valleys. Some parents are morning people. Some are night people. Everybody's heard these expressions. They mean that people have different energy responses to phases of the day. If you're the type who doesn't come to life till noon, no amount of will power is going to make you very productive after breakfast. Your body simply says no. It is important to get to know your physical highs and lows, and if you're lucky and able, to schedule your work according to these peaks and dips of energy.

Exhaustion often can be prevented easily enough by taking care of your health. Getting proper food, rest, exercise, eliminating cigarettes and excessive alcoholic beverages, all help. You might even throw in a vitamin tablet.

As I mentioned before, I found conflict to be very destructive of energy. I wish I had a pat solution for how to deal with this. I don't. Being human, every parent is going to have situations come up which will be adverse—one person in opposition to what the other one wants to do. There's no easy way out of conflict. In fact, when the children get older, there's no way out at all, except for compromise. We have to come to terms with it—or, if it's a motorcycle, ride with it—with common sense and patience. The alternative is misery and continual exhaustion.

A final thought about energy depletion is the need to evaluate our physical condition honestly. If our go-power becomes gone-power, are we actually letting this happen to us; and if so, why?

Are you overworking as a way to put off needed thinking about your life and to avoid decision making?

Are you allowing yourself to become exhausted from your life's responsibilities as a way of excusing yourself from making any changes in your personal life?

Is your exhaustion simply due to an ignorance, probably inexcusable, about what causes energy to be used well and what drains it?

Is your continual "I'm busy, overworked and exhausted" your way of protecting yourself from facing your need to meet new people, make new friends, and in particular, form new heterosexual relationships?

Each of us faces the possibility of a personal energy crisis, but it is a malady which can be avoided by introducing effective preventive measures.

If, after an honest evaluation of your life, you still need a 30-hour day to keep yourself and family going, the best I can do is offer you hope and quote the bible again, "And this, too, shall pass."

I know. I've got the care, feeding and educating of four of my children behind me. I've only got two to go. Any day now my energy crisis should be strictly memories.

Appendix
From Survival to Growth

On my 10th anniversary as a single parent, I looked in the mirror and saw not only my reflection but the images of the difficult decade now behind me. My face was young enough for a woman in her late 40's but my eyes were unmistakably old. Yet, the tightness I used to see so often as I put on my makeup in the morning, before leaving to meet "the public" was gone. My old eyes looked peaceful and my face was soft.

I celebrated my anniversary by tallying up some of the hurdles I had successfully overcome and admitting a few I still battled.

Certainly, I had come through my need to be defensive. Ten years earlier, when divorce was hardly within the frame of reference for Catholics, my decision to move out of my home and raise the children alone was looked upon with shock by our family acquaintances. Since we had met most of these people through various church organizations, that was an understandable reaction. However, I found it difficult to accept the insensitive questions I was asked, such as, "If you had tried harder, don't you think you could have saved your marriage?" "How could you turn your back on God by defiling

His holy sacrament?" "Didn't you agree to stay married for better or for worse?" "If you had made a Marriage Encounter, don't you think that would have saved your marriage?"

When questions like these were asked, I reacted defensively and angrily. I had no intention of talking about private aspects of my marriage relationship. It was nobody's business. I didn't want to be criticized or condemned. I wanted to be admired for my courage to do the difficult but necessary thing I had done. I wanted people to pat me on the back and say, "You did the right thing."

Ten years later, having the approval of others was just not important to me any more. I had placed my confidence in my conscience and made a difficult decision which turned out to be justified. The proof of this was my personal and family life. In these 10 years, I had progressed to where the only approval I needed for my actions was my own.

After my entry into single parenthood, I did experience a change in one aspect of my personality. I had always been an almost excessively patient person, very understanding of others and always able to react to unkindness by wondering, "But what's *their* side of the story?" I was really hung up on "There go I but for the grace of God," and I was, with little effort, patient and nonjudgmental.

When I assumed the responsibilities of total parenthood, I found that patience was no longer a natural virtue. I had to work at it now. Worse, I would find sudden hostilities surge up in me, triggered very easily by an incident, remark or commentary I would interpret as critical of me individually or of one-parent families in general.

One time my sudden hostility was almost humorous. I had just begun working at a new job at the State University of New York at Stony Brook when I received an invitation to join the Stony Brook Women's Club. Their invitation was addressed to "Mrs. Paul Bosco." Paul is my oldest son. My name has never been connected with his, though I had the house phone listed in the directory in his name. The best I could figure out was that someone matched my address in the telephone book, listed under Paul's name, and assumed I was his wife. Rather than addressing me by my own name, they chose to marry me off, obviously a higher status than being a single, professional woman. My hostility soared.

Making no attempt to be reasonable about my anger, I declined the invitation with a curt note that said something like: "Obviously, this is a *wive's* club, not a women's club, and therefore not for me. I would also like to point out that in addressing me as Mrs. Paul Bosco, you have made me guilty of incest, since Paul is my son."

Today I would never respond in such a way. I'd have a good laugh and probably accept the invitation. As I developed more confidence in my life, more self-approval, and began to see that good results were happening in my one-parent family, I relaxed enough so that angers and resentments softened. My sudden hostilities were caused as much by my own up-tightness as by insensitive others.

After 10 years, I also have learned to deal with my own restlessness, becoming aware that this is caused by internal disconnections rather than external situations. Restlessness stemmed more from hanging on to unreal hopes and expectations than from the actual tedium and frustrations of the new life. Where once I had hoped to see myself as a wife—loved, cared for, protected, assisted and at-goal; I now had to revise that picture of myself to—person alone, strong, on own two feet, at the mercy of all life's elements unprotected, unassisted and with shifting goals. Once I reorganized and rearranged my one-time hopes and expectations, the restlessness greatly calmed down.

After 10 years, other problems are not yet settled. I still find a lot of loneliness; little let-up in the responsibility burden; financial demands which still make it impossible for me to stop moonlighting or to buy something frivolous on impulse; and occasional fatigue. However, I do have a better perspective on this. Who's lonelier—me, without a husband; or my sister Rosemary, watching the husband she loves deteriorate slowly from Parkinson's Disease? Who's poorer—me, without the money for a trip; or the couple who just spent their savings to cover legal fees for their teenage son in trouble from drug abuse? Who's more tired—me, because I worked 10 hours today; or my neighbor's mother, 8 years older than myself, who sat in the house all day because she has no skills to get a job?

The old-fashioned expression for a better perspective on life was "count your blessings." I've re-learned to do that and it's a good-sense habit that makes for good health all around.

After these many years, I still feel an occasional overwhelming dismalness about life. At these times, I'm dangerously in touch with the Peggy Lee number—"Is That All There Is?" or with Michael Caine, "What's It All About, Alfie?"

The gloom, uninvited and unwanted, hangs over me, like the shroud that it is, and I get stuck in Why? We're born, we live, struggle, suffer, give birth and die; and then our children live, struggle, suffer, give birth and die. What a senseless joke! I get yearning about wanting out of this whole, crazy, insane scene. So I get myself out of the house and focus on communicating with other people and before I realize it, the dismalness is gone and I am glad.

These times are not the exclusive pain of single parents. Dismalness is part of the human condition, not confined to any one group. I don't know what triggers the attack. I do know that the mood is insidious and evil, for it temporarily makes life a lie, when life is not a lie at all. Life is a connection of love—begun when the Source set the sharing of life into motion—that has transcended and will continue to transcend the centuries. Life is the only real truth.

When the vision of life gets narrowed into tiny cycles that end, no wonder dismalness sets in. I'm inclined to think that the vision of life narrows when we begin to focus too much on our selves. When we harbor thoughts, even unconsciously, too long focused on our own hard times, our deprivations, our failures, our "bad luck", whatever, we're set up for dismalness. Yet, when the attack is on, I've learned that knowing the cause is far less important than finding the escape from dismalness and restoration of confidence in life and love. Forgetting myself and focusing on something outside nyself is usually my escape hatch from this deadliness.

After a decade of singlehood, I still find now-and-then boredom in this state of life. Sometimes I have to admit I'm very dull company for myself. I'll yearn for a break in the pattern, or for something exciting to come along in my life.

I, like everyone else, have to find my own devises for blocking boredom, which, again, I describe not as having a shortage of work or time on my hands, but rather as heaviness, lack of stimulation, too few successes, not enough change, and the absence of a mate, a friend, a counterpart or other person who welcomes your communication.

The greatest gift I have found after these difficult years is peace.

You may think I'm saying peace and meaning quiet, tranquility, lack of motion, stillness—virtually a cessation of life. Not at all. That is not peace. Peace is not quiet. It is active, creative, exciting, full of rebirths and discoveries of self. Peace can be defined properly only by thinking of its opposite—conflict, battles, war. This, unfortunately, is the description of the living environment of too many people, particularly those caught in a marriage disruption. To find peace is to conquer the conflicts within yourself, putting your life in order, getting rid of built-in angers.

You may wonder what I mean when I talk about getting rid of conflict. After all, daily living brings conflict—your watch breaks in the morning; your car needs a new battery; your child's doing poorly in school and teacher is blaming you . . .

These are, however, manageable conflicts, happening outside yourself and fixable, if inconvenient and annoying.

The peace I am talking about is the real and pervading sense of knowing you have overcome the internal conflicts—that you are going to get from A to B without hitting a brick wall, that you have gotten rid of the obstacles and now you can make progress and move ahead.

Peace doesn't come without a price. Years ago, when Archbishop Fulton Sheen was a television personality, I remember his referring to human spiritual achievement as a work of art, produced out of pain. His analogies were that metal must be pounded and hammered before it becomes a fine sculpture, and marble must be chiseled before you get a Pieta. And so it is with human beings. Suffering, difficulties and hard years hurt, but they can also shape us into compassionate, understanding, non-judgmental, good people, at peace with the world and ourselves—if we let them.

From my experiences, I have concluded that single

parents must go through several stages to achieve growth and peace, beyond survival.

1. We have to admit our disruption. If the situation is bad, look at it honestly and admit it. One widow was afraid to admit how miserable and frightened she was after her husband died because she thought she'd be sinning if she complained about an act she saw as "God's Will." Her energies went into denying her misery rather than picking up the pieces of her life and reestablishing a healthy family environment.

In my own case, I tried for years to convince myself that I was carrying out God's will by trying to make a go of a destructive marriage. I tried to believe what the marriage ceremony stated, that when the sacrifice is complete, love is perfect. But one May day, when I was trying to care for an infant and four children under eight, with a phlebitis the size of a large egg on my ankle, unable to walk and doing my duties by crawling from room to room, having a husband who told me these were *my* problems, not his, I had to face the truth that, in the light of this reality, I could no longer play with words like "sacrifice" and "perfect love."

We stay immobilized until we admit that we're dealing with disruption. Once we face this truth, then we can move on to the next necessities—

2. We have to move beyond our anger, resentments and hostilities;

3. We have to fight, if necessary, for survival, forcing the changes in our lives that might put us back into health and order. When I moved out of my home, taking my children with me, that was my first round in the fight for survival;

4. We have to develop tremendous endurance;

5. We have to get through an acceptance-rejection phase, where we deal with our guilt, our self-destructive images, our shock at the demands and negative status of our new position; develop self-confidence, assertiveness, and discover some lanterns in the darkness;

6. Finally, we go beyond survival, reaching growth and a rebirth into peace. This happens as some of the pressures lift, successes are achieved, and we find a contentment with our achievement, for it is notable. We have given love and family closeness to our children—the good life itself.

Those six stages to achieving growth beyond survival as a single parent are a smoother passage if you recognize the blocking obstacles on the roadway.

I found a major obstacle to growth to be bad early training about love and marriage, particularly for girls, giving us unreal expectations about romance, life and happiness. We're led to believe, à la fairy tales, that our prince is going to come along, give us a kiss and put us smack into happy-ever-after. I remember that on my wedding day, I was dazzled by the thought that I was never going to be lonely again. Now I would have a husband to ease my aloneness. All too soon I experienced loneliness worse than I ever had before because now it was highlighted by dashed, but unreal, expectations.

If we think about this idea of love and marriage—where some enchanted evening someone looks at you across a crowded room and all is well forever—we've really produced a myth. It says that someone else is going to take responsibility for us, be our tranquilizer, make our lives easier.

That is not the way life really is. We each have to work for happiness. It can't be placed on us or given to us by decree. The shining knight on the white horse, or the handsome stranger who smiles at us across a crowded room doesn't exist, and can't hand us happy-ever-after neatly tied with a ribbon. We have to make our own happiness in the situation where we find ourselves.

Another fundamental facet of growth is accepting responsibility for our own actions. We're a great nation of buck passers, suffering from a Put-The-Blame-On-Mame syndrome. I suppose it started with Eve when she put the blame on the serpent as she chewed away at the apple. We have become accustomed to pulling the shades down on our roles in the things that happen to us, in the direction our lives have taken. We can make more good things happen than we realize by making decisions based on our interests and personal pursuit of happiness. We don't have to be passive persons, following the dictates of others or falling into the laissez-faire condition of just letting things happen to us. We *can* take a course, attend a play, make new friends, leave the children in the care of others once in a while.

Right now I am making something new happen in my life. I am selling my house and moving with my youngest son to an apartment. Some people can't figure out why I am doing such a thing, giving up my comfortable living quarters, my fireplace, my park-like yard. My decision isn't based on what others understand. I have come to a new level in my life, where my parent-focused days are coming to an end. I am confronting myself as a different person, with a need for personal self-development taking a priority over parenting. If I am going to allow myself to be open to new activities, new opportunities, maybe travel for the first time in my life, I need more freedom. At this stage, the house ties me to it and I want to move away from this encumbrance.

Will I be successful at making the tremendous adjustment from house living to apartment living? I don't know. Will I be sorry after I give up my house that has so much of me in it—the panelling I chose, the rugs I selected, the trees I planted? I don't know. But I am making the decision and taking responsibility for its outcome. If it turns out to be a mistake, I won't be able to blame anyone or anything else for it. I'm inclined to think I wouldn't even blame myself. I would chalk it up to growing pains, grateful that I learned to take responsibility for my own decisions.

Another crucial ingredient of growth is to learn to be in control of the things you want. If our desires control us, we're immobilized. Like most people, I have what is commonly known as "champagne taste on a beer income." I could so easily be seduced by House Beautiful and living as Lady Gorgeous. But if I spent my time becoming empty because I can't have these costly goodies, I would be immobilized and miserable.

I give credit to my religious training for putting common sense into me at an early age, teaching me that a person becomes truly free only after learning to control his or her desires for the things not within reach. It makes no more sense to become miserable over looking at the same curtains for three years than it does to fret because you're five feet tall when you'd like to be five feet five. Controlling our wants brings contentment—a prerequisite for dissolving conflicts and finding peace.

A single parent's growth is sometimes made more difficult because we're trying to rush it. After my friend Joan's husband left her unexpectedly, she plunged into non-stop work, saying she would keep herself so busy, she wouldn't have time to think about her misery. One day she collapsed into what was labelled a nervous breakdown, becoming severely depressed and needing immediate medical attention. She had tried and failed at rushing into a new life before the old one was resolved.

Entry into single parenthood is almost always a traumatic change from one style of life into another, most often triggered by the shattering events of death or divorce. We have to understand that a healing process has to take place, and this can't be rushed. If you have an operation, you know it takes time to heal. We've undergone surgery, too, the alteration of our lives. While our wounds are not visible, they are, nevertheless, bleeding. In the early period of single parenthood, the pain will recur frequently. We should expect this to happen and not overreact in fear that we'll never get away from the discomforting feelings.

In time, the wounds heal, and one day you find the pain is gone, even though scars remain.

The greatest gift in clearing our way to growth and peace is love. The surest strength and blessing in the life of a single parent stems from the love that surrounds us because we live together with our children. We know what we're working for. We are not really alone, but united in love to our children. As I said before, I keep a banner posted which says, "Unless you love someone, nothing makes sense." In accepting the responsibilities of parenthood alone, we are in the position of filling our lives with love—making very good sense out of our existence.

Growth can be stifled if we are trying to pretend we are superhuman, and so it is important for a single parent to stay honest always, not denying our legitimate needs. Sometimes we're going to have yearnings that won't be eased by chiding ourselves, or telling ourselves to "count blessings", or reminding ourselves that we are lucky because we have the children to love. At times, very human desires will tantalize us—a need to be loved as a man or woman instead of as a parent; a need sometimes for a sexual expression of love; a need to look attractive, feel well, be waited on, to be un-pressured and well rested. I haven't got a formula for how to deal with these needs. I only know we have to admit them, without feeling guilty about them. We are only flesh and blood, and God, Himself, made us this way.

Finally, we have to realize that even after we have put our lives in order and are growing again, in peace, there will be gullies in between the high spots. Life does not come with guarantees. The best way to handle setbacks is with patience, the determination to fight again and survive, and a sense of humor.

One woman, age 27, raising a three-year-old alone, had struggled to come through severe depression, had a good job working as a counsellor in a cancer research project, and felt she was finally living again. Then suddenly, she was stricken with tuberculosis, an old disease, now almost unheard of. She felt defeated as she lay in an isolation room in the hospital, convinced she was destined to be a victim of various injustices forever. Yet, with the help of her family and the knowledge that she had come through a bad time before, she found the confidence and strength to fight back and avoid depression. She has now returned to work and is regaining optimism about life.

Very personally, I think surviving and growing in the face of a difficult life situation requires something else, a very special gift on the soul level, a belief in the Mystery that brought us life and sustains us. Some call this "faith." The best back-up I can relate for how I define this Mystery comes not from a theologian, but a distinguished biologist, Dr. Bentley Glass. Last year, in a lecture, Dr. Glass said one thing which stomped my brain, like God knocking.

He said that if all the sperm that resulted in the birth of the 2½ to 3 billion people on this earth right now could be collected, this sperm would fit into a four-ounce container. And if all the eggs were similarly collected, these would fill a one and one-half pint container. In other words, *all the life-beginnings and all the coding that determines everything about a person, from the color of eyes to personality, for all the people now on this planet, could be held in the palm of a hand.*

I get a kind of high in the face of that Mystery—an incredible sense of being linked to Something unfathomable and magnificent.

I may continue to feel bewildered, terrified at times, confused about the next step in the continuing saga of what I want to be and what I'm going to try to be as I'm still "growing up."

But I stop feeling alone.

That, plus six kids and a lot of hard work, has bought me a ticket to happiness.

I have never been able to think up a better destination.